CHARISMATIC RENEWAL

CHARISMATIC RENEWAL
Reflections of a Pastor

by
John B. Healey

PAULIST PRESS
New York/Paramus/Toronto

Library of Congress
Catalog Card Number: 76-9368

ISBN: 0-8091-1948-X

Published by Paulist Press
Editorial Office: 1865 Broadway, N.Y., N.Y. 10023
Business Office: 400 Sette Drive, Paramus, N.J. 07652

Printed and bound in the
United States of America

Contents

Foreword

In the present work, CHARISMATIC RE-NEWAL: REFLECTIONS OF A PASTOR, Father John B. Healey has made a significant contribution to contemporary spirituality. Effectively in matter and engagingly in manner he has given a brief yet apt account of the origins, the resurgence, and the directions of the modern charismatic movement. Happily free from technical jargon, it is within the easy comprehension of the average reader. Father Healey's clear, bland and irenic approach will do much to dispel any of the antipathy to the program that is based on misinformation or misconception.

The movement is not a fad nor are its adherents fanatics or eccentrics. From the beginning there have been charismatic, equally with hierarchical, tendencies in the Church. In 1 Thessalonians 5:19 St. Paul has clearly expressed this, "Do not restrain the Holy Spirit; do not despise inspired messages."

Calmly and reasonably the author sets forth the basis of the charismatic experience, namely, God acting in everyday life. The movement is by no means elitist or esoteric, looking on non-participants as the less-favored masses. The representative charismatic will say: "I don't feel that I am better than you, but I know I am better than I was." The emotions and the imagination are integral and essential parts of the human psyche and should be recognized in prayer and worship. Too little heed for too long has been paid to the enduring and honorable tradition of ascetical and mystical theology. These belong not only to the votary in the cloistered cell but also to the man and woman in the pew and even in the street. The charismatics have been drawn to a greater awareness of the presence of the Eucharist. To be noted is the fact that charism and Eucharist share a common root that means gift, grace or favor. As the Eucharist is the gift of Christ so is the charism the gift of the Holy Spirit.

With admirable restraint and plausibility, Father Healey has discussed the difficult questions of prophecy and speaking in tongues. Of equal merit is his treatment of prayer, emotion in religion and the relationship of the priest to the charismatic group.

The words of the beautiful Sequence of Pentecost are highly appropriate to the charismatic movement:

> "What is parched, fructify.
> What is rigid, gently bend.
> What is frozen, warmly tend."

Most Reverend Francis J. Mugavero
Bishop of Brooklyn
February 25, 1976

Introduction:
The Spirit Today

There are signs everywhere today that the Holy Spirit is acting powerfully among men and women and that they are responding. We believe that He has been present and active among Christians in a special way since the first Pentecost, that He guided the Chosen People before that, and that He is active in the life of every man and woman who has ever lived. But something special is happening today.

Human Response

The action of God always takes into account the free response of men and women to His grace. This explains why although the Spirit works unceasingly and deeply in human life, the effectiveness and manifestation of His presence and action will vary in depth and extent at every moment of human history. The source of both our greatest glory and deepest shame is this: that, individually and collectively, we are able to cooperate with Almighty God in the creation of the next moment of our existence.

"Forgotten Person"

It is clear to us now that, for a variety of historical, theological and sociological reasons, the presence and action of the Holy Spirit have been obscured and neglected in Christian thought and life in recent centuries, especially in the Western Church. Not long ago the Spirit was sometimes referred to among us as "the forgotten Person of the Trinity."

Spirit Reveals Jesus

While His presence is still as silent and mysterious as ever, His effectiveness is no longer obscure. For it is the work of the Spirit, not to draw attention to Himself, but to reveal Jesus to us. This is precisely what He is doing today. Daily the number increases of those who are coming to know Jesus as Lord in their personal lives. And this they are proclaiming increasingly in word and deed. Scripture tells us that this is the work of the Holy Spirit.

In Individual Lives

The cult of the Holy Spirit is increasing everywhere in the Church, and on every level. It is in our individual lives, however, that the Spirit is most manifest, in the gifts of love, joy, peace, prayerfulness, prophecy, healing, tongues, increasing love for the Eucharist and for Scripture. Everywhere more Christians are awakening to an awareness and appreciation of what we are and of the place of Jesus Christ in our daily lives. For many, no longer does He remain on the periphery of their existence, worshiped for a brief while on Sundays and then "called upon" otherwise only when there is some need. Increasingly Christians everywhere are growing in their capacity to sing a continuous hymn of praise and thanksgiving, and at last know the reality of our ancient liturgical refrain: "Rejoice in the Lord always; again I say, rejoice" (Phil. 4:4).

"God Has No Grandchildren"

Everyone who believes that Jesus is Lord does so only by the power of the Spirit. Every Christian may relate to the Paraclete in an intimate, personal way by virtue of his or her Baptism and Confirmation. Someone recently remarked: "God has no grandchildren." How true. For each of us is His precious child in our own right. And when we gather together in the Name of Jesus, that is, when we become a People of God, a Church, how much more powerfully does the Spirit come upon us—as once He did in the Upper Room.

Charismatic Renewal

The power of the Holy Spirit is very much in evidence among us today in what is called the Charismatic Renewal. These chapters are an attempt to give some initial insight into this new phenomenon on the Catholic scene. It is my hope that those who attend charismatic prayer-meetings will gain from them a deeper appreciation of what they already accept. Those who are interested or curious or perhaps opposed to the Renewal will, it is also hoped, find in these chapters a sympathetic presentation of both its positive and negative aspects.

The ideas expressed here are entirely those of the author, based upon his own experience and reflection. That too is the whole weight of their authority. These chapters are meant to be mostly expository, although they are occasionally exhortatory, the result of the author's own deep involvement and desire to share what he has found most worthwhile. He believes he has done this with restraint.

These chapters are not intended to be polemical in any sense. If others see and interpret aspects of the Renewal differently, this will only add to the understanding of something that is affecting the lives of many Christians today. Just as the Charismatic Renewal is new and growing, so also are its underlying theological and philosophical premises being gradually developed and examined. Perhaps these chapters may add a little even to this development. If so, this will be only another proof that "the Spirit breathes where He will" (Jn. 3:8).

We are grateful to Mr. Don Zirkel, editor of *The Tablet,* Catholic weekly of the Diocese of Brooklyn, for allowing us to use material that appeared in its columns under the author's by-line.

1.
The Present Situation

At the present time hundreds of thousands of Catholics attend charismatic prayer meetings in the United States. The number keeps growing.

What distinguishes these groups is: emphasis on praising Jesus Christ as Lord, use of the gifts (charisms) of the Holy Spirit (including the more exceptional ones of healing, prophecy and speaking in tongues), spontaneous prayer, commitment to this style of worship, and fidelity to one's particular prayer-group.

Effects

Those involved attest frequently to these effects in their personal lives: a distinct change in their Christian orientation, new awareness of the presence and action of Jesus in daily life, deeper insight into Scripture with an increased desire to read it, greater desire to spend time in prayer, a sense of peace and joy, enthusiasm for the things of the Lord, and greater love for the Eucharist and for the Church.

What About It?

What about the Charismatic Renewal in the Catholic Church? How does one account for Catholics becoming involved in religious practice so different from that to which we are accustomed? What are the positive aspects of the Charismatic Renewal? What are its dangers? These are some of the questions I will deal with in these chapters.

Two Statements

Let us begin with two recent statements on the Renewal. On January 22, 1975, the U.S. Bishops' Committee for Pastoral Research and Practices published its "Statement on Catholic Charismatic Renewal." It concludes with these words: "To the members of the movement, then, to pastors, and to all the faithful of Christ, we commend the words of Scripture, which we take as our own guiding light: 'Do not stifle the Spirit. Do not despise prophecies. Test everything; retain what is good. Avoid any semblance of evil' (1 Thess. 5:19-22). We encourage those who already belong, and we support the positive and desirable directions of the Charismatic Renewal."

At about the same time, Religious News Service (which is published by National Conference of Christians and Jews) reported: "Generally speaking there is no question that the charismatic movement has now emerged as a full-blown religious revival, not only within the established Churches of the U.S. but in many areas of the world. And that emergence —by its very nature a challenge to church traditions and practices—is attested to by the widespread attention and controversy it has engendered."

From these statements we see that the Charismatic Renewal: (1) is a contemporary reality that is challenging widely held Christian attitudes and practices, (2) has the support and encouragement of the committee appointed by the National Conference of

Catholic Bishops to examine it, and (3) is controversial.

Strong Opinions

Most Catholics have strong opinions about Charismatic Renewal, one way or the other. This is understandable. There is much about it that is properly left to one's devotional taste and to one's legitimate theological viewpoint. Where taste is concerned, some are repelled by a style of religious worship that is so much at variance with our own long-standing practices.

Main Theological Problem

Perhaps the most serious and fundamental theological problem that the Charismatic Renewal presents for many Catholics is whether or not God acts directly in human life. Does He enter into the "nitty-gritty" of our daily lives in a personal, loving way, or does He only deal with us through "secondary causes"? Although Scripture is filled with accounts of direct interaction between God and man, Christian thinking has come so far from this that it is today an axiom of modern theology that men must infer their knowledge of God from events of this world and not from any direct experience of the divine. For generations Catholic theological training has been such that, while we admit the possibility of religious (mystical) experience and its validity in the lives of the Saints, it is a priori suspect for ordinary Christians.

Whom To Believe?

Today, however, increasing numbers of Catholics attest that God is acting directly in their everyday lives, and that the fruits of the Holy Spirit are manifest to them. They are convinced that they have experienced a new relationship with God which is radically changing for the better their human and Christian relationships. Among these are bishops, priests, religious, laymen and women, from the most diverse backgrounds, young and old, highly educated and unlettered. Are they to be believed?

These chapters, then, will concern themselves with something of great importance to the life of the Church. Many good Catholics are deeply involved in charismatic prayer-meetings. No one, especially teachers and leaders, can afford to be apathetic about them.

The Renewal is either the work of the Holy Spirit or it is not. If it is not, it ought to be quickly eradicated. If it is the work of the Holy Spirit, it should be encouraged and guided.

2.
What Is the
Charismatic Renewal?

The Charismatic Renewal is a complex phenomenon. 1. *Sociologically*, as Father Joseph Fichter S. J. points out in his book, *The Catholic Cult of the Paraclete*, the fact of increasing numbers of Christians meeting regularly for spontaneous prayer is inexplicable in terms of recent patterns of religious practice in the U. S. 2. *Spiritually*, many believe that it is the "new Pentecost" for which Pope John XXIII asked all Christians to pray before Vatican II. 3. *Theologically*, the Renewal is based upon and emphasizes fundamental doctrines of Christianity. We will deal briefly here with the third aspect.

Theologically Central

The Charismatic Renewal is not an intrusion of new and alien elements into orthodox Christianity, nor is it simply another popular devotion suitable to the temporary needs of the Church at a particular time. It is concerned with basic Christianity as described in the New Testament. In Acts and the letters of Paul, the Church is shown as a community of believers in the Risen Christ, who is Lord of their lives by the power and action of the Holy Spirit. "No one can say 'Jesus is Lord' unless he is under the influence of the Holy Spirit" (1 Cor. 12:3).

11

To proclaim, by the power of the Spirit, that Jesus is Lord is at the heart of what it means to be Christian. To emphasize this proclamation today in prayer and in action is the purpose and goal of the Charismatic Renewal. This can be accomplished only through "the influence of the Holy Spirit," that is, by the use of His gifts.

Change over the Centuries

Over the centuries, however, we Christians have somehow come to believe that the gifts of the Spirit, especially those of healing, prophecy and speaking in tongues, were intended by God only for the first years of the Church. And so, the charismatic (gift) dimension of the Church has long been obscured.

Structure of Church

In its essential structure, however, the Church is no less charismatic than it is hierarchical and sacramental. The abiding presence and action of the Holy Spirit in all the members of the Body of Christ in every age is as fundamental and integral a doctrine of Christianity as are the Incarnation, the seven Sacraments, or the teaching authority of Pope and bishops.

"There is one God and Father of all men, who is Lord of all, works through all, and is in all. Each one of us has been given a special gift, in proportion to what Christ has given. . . . He did this to prepare all God's people for the work of Christian service, to build up the Body of Christ" (Eph. 4:5, 12). To deny, then, to the Church the "special gift(s)" that belong to "all God's People" is not to "build up the Body of Christ," but to devitalize it and to immobilize the action of the Spirit.

Vatican II

The *Constitution on the Church* of Vatican II says about charismatic gifts: "It is not only through the Sacraments and Church ministries that the same Holy Spirit sanctifies and leads the People of God and enriches it with virtues. Allotting His gifts 'to everyone according as He will' (1 Cor. 12:11), He distributes special graces among the faithful of every rank . . . for the renewal and upbuilding of the Church. . . . These charismatic gifts, whether they be the most outstanding or the more simple and widely diffused, are to be received with thanksgiving and consolation, for they are exceedingly suitable and useful for the needs of the Church" (n. 12).

Christian Means Charismatic

All Christians, then, are "charismatic." While all the baptized receive gifts of the Spirit, their use depends on our cooperation. Therefore, their manifestation will vary. They were abundantly evident in Apostolic times, as Scripture attests, especially when Christians gathered to praise Jesus as Lord. This is happening again in charismatic prayer-meetings.

The gifts of the Spirit are intended to be used, not merely analyzed. Accepting the gifts today is basically a matter of one's personal faith. Attending a charismatic prayer-meeting in a spirit of prayerfulness and openness will effect, through the Spirit, what inquiry and analysis by themselves can never bring about.

3.
The Renewal and Catholic Life

Bishops' Statement

In their "Statement on Charismatic Renewal" of January 22, 1975, the Committee of the National Conference of Catholic Bishops wrote: "Many of those who belong to the movement experience a new sense of spiritual values, a heightened consciousness of the action of the Holy Spirit, the praise of God and a deepening personal commitment to Christ. Many, too, have grown in devotion to the Eucharist and partake more fruitfully in the sacramental life of the Church. Reverence for the Mother of the Lord takes on fresh meaning and many feel a deeper sense of attachment to the Church" (n. 5).

Depth and Meaning

What the Bishops' Committee stated is borne out by theological inquiry, which reveals that the Charismatic Renewal not only is situated in the mainstream of Catholic doctrine, liturgy and ascetical teaching, but adds depth and meaning to each of these dimensions in the ongoing spiritual life of a growing number of Catholics.

Three Directions

My own experience and that of many others in

the Renewal bear witness to personal Christian growth especially in these ways:

1. *doctrinally*, by increased understanding of and personal devotion to the Holy Trinity;

2. *liturgically*, by increased love for the Eucharist and an eagerness to participate in its Liturgy;

3. *ascetically*, by leading us into a spiritual "way of life."

I. THE TRINITY

Like all Christians I have always accepted the Trinity as the most sublime mystery of our faith. I have understood, accepted and been grateful that Jesus has revealed God to us as a loving Father. Likewise I have accepted and been thankful that the Holy Spirit continues since Pentecost to reveal Jesus to us in all that He said and did while on earth, and that the Spirit guides the Church in truth. Mostly, however, I have tried to relate myself to Jesus who I believe is present to us in the Eucharist, in the Mystical Body, in the living Word, etc.

Trinitarian Spirituality

While I tried to accept each Person into my spiritual life as sincerely and as deeply as I was able, I confess that this remained for me almost entirely on the level of my intellect. Although I often wished it were otherwise, I can honestly say that not until recently did I experience a personal relationship to the Father and the Spirit as distinct Persons from Jesus. Through my involvement with others in the Charismatic Renewal I can now say that, however poorly developed it still remains, my devotional practice has become truly trinitarian. Jesus, the Father and the Spirit have each become a real Person to me.

Through Prayer

This has come about through prayer, of course, but through prayer in a particular way. I found that as I opened myself daily to the action of the Spirit in union with others and when alone (and these two ways support and enhance each other), Jesus is presently being "revealed" to me more intimately as *Jesus*. To explain this further is difficult, except to say that it is much more than intellectual. The best way I know to put it is to say that, to a degree, I now know Jesus in the way that a person knows someone he loves.

God Is My Father

As I come to know Jesus more intimately, I perceive a new and deep understanding and love of God the Father as *my* Father, the one who created, sustains and cares for me personally. It bears out what Jesus said to Philip: "To have seen Me is to have seen the Father" (Jn. 14:9).

The Spirit Becomes Manifest

As Jesus and the Father become more "real" Persons to me by the action of the Spirit, so also, paradoxically, does the Spirit make His presence felt more distinctly. This is in accord with what St. John writes: "We *know* that He (Jesus) lives in us by the Spirit that He has given us" (1 Jn. 3:24). Indeed, wherever Jesus is, there the Spirit is at work. Jesus Himself was conceived when the Spirit overshadowed Mary. His public ministry began only after

He was empowered for it by the Spirit in the Jordan. The Church came into being on Pentecost when the disciples and Mary were each filled by the Spirit with gifts and power.

Jesus, Spirit, Church, Gifts

So it remains today. Wherever Jesus is united to man, individually or in community, there the Spirit is at work with His gifts to effect this unity. Jesus, Spirit, Church and the gifts of the Spirit are inseparably linked in Christian life.

All Four in Renewal

These four constituent elements of Christian life are clearly seen together today in charismatic prayer-meetings and in the spirituality of most of those who attend these meetings. Father Herbert Mühlen writes: "Whenever we see and hear other men expressing their deep inner devotion to God in praise and prayer, then we see and hear something of the Spirit of God Himself, who is acting in them and they in Him" (*The Holy Spirit and Power*, ed. by Kilian McDonnell, O.S.B., p. 112). He writes further: "The theological implications of the Charismatic Renewal are trinitarian in a way which is scarcely duplicated in any other aspect of systematic theology" (p. 112).

II. THE EUCHARIST

In all truly Catholic belief and practice the Sacrament of the Eucharist holds a central place. An unmistakable and indispensable criterion for the acceptability of any doctrine or devotional practice that calls itself Catholic is this: Does it lead one to greater Eucharistic understanding, love and devotion?

Prayer-Meeting Leads to Eucharist

In my experience I have found that involvement in the Charismatic Renewal leads naturally to a deeper, more joyful, more devout and more efficacious participation in Eucharistic celebration. A charismatic prayer-meeting, indeed, has its own purpose within itself, namely, to praise Jesus as Lord spontaneously by the use of the gifts of the Spirit within a communal context for the "building up of the Body of Christ" (Eph. 4:12). Nevertheless, the prayer and the praise of the meeting prepare Catholics individually and together for more fruitful participation in Eucharistic celebration. The dispositions of faith, praise, joy and expectancy engendered in the meeting are carried over and intensified in the Liturgy. Occasionally the prayer-meeting constitutes the Liturgy of the Word.

Priests and the Eucharist

This natural progression from prayer-meeting to Eucharist is perhaps most evident whenever priests who are involved or interested in the Renewal convene in any numbers for retreats, days of renewal, etc. I have heard many priests, young and old alike, witness to the unity and power of the priesthood that they have experienced in these settings. I recall one such noteworthy gathering at the College of Steubenville, Ohio, in June, 1975. More than five hundred priests and a few bishops joined daily in Eucharistic Liturgies wherein the gifts of the Spirit to individual priests were most manifest. Again, the annual retreats for priests held at Mount Augustine on Staten Island, N.Y. are occasions of Eucharistic celebrations that deeply affect all who attend. The annual national meetings at Notre Dame and elsewhere are regularly climaxed by most joyous Eucharistic celebrations.

III. SPIRITUAL WAY OF LIFE

Involvement in the Charismatic Renewal leads one gradually into what amounts to a spiritual way of life. For some it is their first direct confrontation with their own spiritual selves in a continuous way. In the past we Catholics, if we took our spiritual life seriously at all, were content to be guided from outside ourselves, mostly through sermons and occasional spiritual reading. Very few of us conferred regularly with a spiritual director. Usually the sum total of our devotional practice was attendance at Mass, prayers at regular times and when in need, and perhaps the Rosary. Fidelity to these devotional "practices" was a sign of religious commitment and depth. Consequently emphasis was on one's own performance. If in all this there was a personal relationship to Jesus, most often it was neither an intimate one nor ongoing in the way one relates to a dear friend.

Religion a Private Matter

Furthermore, spiritual practice was traditionally an individual and private affair. As for shared prayer, liturgical or otherwise, it meant to recite certain memorized prayers together or to follow a common text. In Catholic religious practices there was very little allowance for individual expression.

Presence of God in Community

One who, by God's grace, begins to attend charismatic prayer-meetings regularly, and to become involved in a praying community, enters into direct contact with the presence of God in the community. It is, in a sense, the reversal of the approach to spirituality in which we were educated. We have become accustomed to look first to traditions, doctrines, liturgical forms, hierarchical guidance, etc., and to form our personal spirituality in accord with these. In the Charismatic Renewal the wellspring and focal point of personal spirituality for many is the direct experience of the presence of the living God at prayer-meetings. This leads in turn, especially where there is guidance by those qualified to give it, into greater understanding of and love for the Church, its doctrines and practices.

Effects of Experience of God

Direct experience with the living God has profound effects upon one's spiritual outlook. It can and it has produced extraordinary changes for the better in the religious orientation of many Catholics. As we noted above, the Bishops' Committee listed especially "a new sense of spiritual values, a heightened consciousness of the action of the Holy Spirit, the praise of God and a deepening commitment to Christ." It is my experience and that of many priests and bishops that this is so. The Charismatic Renewal is currently a source of true nourishment to the Church as it now exists.

4.
The Prayer-Meeting

Attendance at prayer-meetings is the best way to understand the Charismatic Renewal. And prayer-meetings must be experienced to be adequately understood. The reason is because this type of shared-prayer engages the total person, not merely our understanding and intellect.

Nevertheless, having said this, it may help some if I describe prayer-meetings as I know them. Others will, of course, be able to add much to what I say, because we are concerned here with a most intimate and personal area: our relationship to God and to others in Christ.

No Two Are Alike

No two prayer-meetings are alike even when the same persons are present. The direction that a particular meeting will take depends upon our sensitivity to the impulses of the Spirit in everyone present. For "there are different gifts but the same Spirit. . . . To each person the manifestation of the Spirit is given for the common good. To one the Spirit gives wisdom in discourse, to another the power to express knowledge. Through the Spirit one receives faith; by the same Spirit another is given the gift of healing; and still another miraculous powers. Prophecy is given to one; to another power to distinguish

one spirit from another. One receives the gift of
tongues, another that of interpreting the tongues.
But it is the same Spirit who produces all these gifts,
distributing them to each as He wills" (1 Cor. 12:4-
11).

The Leader

There is a leader at prayer-meetings. His or her
function is to start the meeting and to guide it sensi-
tively under the inspiration of the Holy Spirit. He or
she interferes as little as possible with the promptings of the Spirit that come through the spontaneous
participation of those present. Consequently he or
she speaks as little as possible, and only when the
common good of the meeting requires it.

The Meeting Begins

To begin, the leader may simply and briefly
state the principal purpose of the meeting (to praise
Jesus as Lord and Savior) and then, perhaps, suggest
a hymn to be sung. There usually follows a period of
silent reflection wherein is experienced the peace and
beauty of the Presence Jesus promised to those
"gathered together in (His) Name" (Mt. 18:20). And
so we begin to "settle down" to an hour or so of
shared worship of Jesus Christ under the guidance of
His Holy Spirit.

The Spirit at Work

It is through our reverent awareness of the
Spirit moving and working among us that we begin
to discern what He is telling us at each meeting. As
the hour progresses, someone may read a passage of
Scripture that strikes him or her as appropriate; an-

other will speak a prayer of thanksgiving to God for His blessings upon self or others; someone may tell of a manifestation of God's favor in the past week; prayers for a special intention may be solicited; occasionally a request is made for a particular hymn to be sung by all; or the leader may suggest that we lift our voices in thanksgiving and praise to God in whatever words or tongue we choose; and there are usually frequent periods of prayerful silence. So the time moves along in faith, in joy, in peace and in love.

The Common Good

While spontaneity and openness are encouraged, no particular person is expected to speak out at any time or for the entire meeting. Everyone learns in time, however, to be solicitous for the "common good" of all at a meeting, as St. Paul advised. For, although each of us has his or her own good reasons for being there, the Apostle tells us that God's gifts are for the "building up of the Body of Christ" (Eph. 4:13), which we ourselves constitute. "We, being many, are one Body in Christ" (Rom. 12:5).

Experience in Learning

The growth of any prayer group is an experience in learning. For although this form of prayer is not new among Christians, as Scripture and history attest, it is currently a novel and unfamiliar experience for most Catholics. So it is that only through a process of effort, trial and error does any group mature and acquire an atmosphere of quiet peace and depth that enables a person to pray with increasingly greater ease and reverence.

Awkward Beginnings

As a cooperative effort of sincere people who are trying to worship God together in a new way, meetings will sometimes possess the awkwardness of any new personal relationship on a deep level. This is especially true of groups which are just starting. For in its growth every group encounters some of the difficulties of cooperation and communication that are found in any family where there is diversity of age, temperament, education and spiritual growth. For the spirituality of prayer-groups is based upon a realistic acceptance of the concrete realities of the members' lives. The power of the Spirit helps us to accept others lovingly as they are; paradoxically, then, natural differences and diversity of gifts are a source of unity in Christ.

Deep Friendship

It is inevitable that shared prayer will plant the seed of deep and meaningful friendships among those who participate. The reason is the nature of friendship. Common interest and activity is the basis of any friendship. The more profound and personal the area of sincere mutual sharing, the deeper the bond of love and friendship that is possible. This is obviously true in marriage whenever a couple is capable of real communication. It is true in study groups and discussion clubs. It is no less true of us who share Christ Himself in praise.

Other Effects

Shared prayer leads inevitably, as well, to greater devotion both in private prayer and in our participation in the Liturgy. There are a number of reasons for this, primarily one's growth in love for Christ and the revitalizing of the gifts of His Spirit received in Baptism and Confirmation. Those who engage in shared prayer, almost without exception, discover within themselves an increased desire to pray privately and liturgically. They learn, too, that the type of prayer that comes most readily to their minds and lips is that of praising and thanking God. The consequence of this is a greater sense of joy and peace in their total living. Mostly, however, there is experienced an increase of the great Gift of Love, without which everything else "profiteth me nothing" (1 Cor. 13:3). Cardinal Suenens wrote recently: "I see the Spirit animating the broad phenomenon of communally shared prayer and behind the many attempts at renewal of the Church through communities radically orienting themselves to the Gospel."

Great Need Today

The experience of unity and love in Christ is, in my opinion, exactly what Christians everywhere are really searching for, if they would only realize it. Most of us are wearied of talking "about" our faith and are hungry for the reality of Jesus in our lives. Some, I am sure, are strong enough, as human beings and as Christians to relate to Christ on a one-to-one basis. But, with the old supports of religion increasingly removed from us, many have a need to share their faith personally with other Christians in order to keep it alive. At present, few Eucharistic Liturgies enable us to do this. Our hope is that more will do so as time passes.

Meeting Regularly Important

The regularity of prayer meetings (usually once

a week) helps greatly, for it takes time to become accustomed to the spontaneity and joy one meets at them. Besides, one usually needs time to gradually recognize, understand and deal with his or her own reactions in this new religious atmosphere. We are often surprised at our own lack of freedom in expressing ourselves. This can be healed only over a period of time.

Strangeness at First

One's first reaction at a prayer-meeting is usually strangeness and confusion. Great peace will often be experienced at a first visit, but a number of things just do not fit into the pattern of our religious experience. Catholics are not accustomed to spontaneous prayer, individual participation on one's own initiative, using Scripture in a pragmatic way, seeing priests assume roles of equality before the Lord in religious matters, the seemingly unorganized nature of a meeting, and especially prophecy, healing and speaking in tongues.

Understanding Grows

It takes several visits to a prayer-meeting to begin to understand what is really going on, that it is really the Holy Spirit who leads each meeting. It takes time to learn to be attentive and sensitive to the work of the Spirit. The Spirit leads each meeting differently. He has something to say to the group each time they convene; there is a "theme" to each meeting which one learns to recognize from the total context of Scripture readings, prayers, teachings, songs, and prophecies, and even in the silences. No two meetings are alike.

Vatican II has re-emphasized for us the traditional teaching of the many ways that Jesus is present to us: the Eucharist, Scripture, the indwelling of the Trinity in each of us, in the Church entirely and in every "two or three" (or more) "gathered in (My) Name." This last presence is especially experienced at prayer-meetings. It manifests itself mostly in peace and joy.

5.
The Appeal of Prayer-Meetings

Christian Community

What is it about charismatic prayer-meetings that makes people return week after week, even in the hot summer months? And what is it that makes them eager to spend long hours together at these meetings? The answer is: community. Very often it is spiritual need that brings them in the first place; but it is the magnetism of the Christian community, the Body of Christ, that keeps them coming back. The experience of being a vital member of a loving Christian community is powerful, especially if one has never experienced it before.

Communication

At charismatic prayer-meetings one enters gradually into deep and satisfying communication and relationship with others in the most important areas of life. We share our common acceptance of Jesus as Lord, our prayer-life, our spiritual aspirations, our hopes and needs, fears and failures. To those who have never communicated with others on this level, the spontaneity, openness and lack of threat at meetings can offer a grace-filled and humanly fulfilling experience.

28

Welcome Contrast

Many who attend meetings find in them a most welcome contrast to most of their other encounters with people. Much in modern life prevents us from relating to one another on a deep level. Even the best of friends very often discuss only superficial and ephemeral matters. It is even expected that in conversation one will stay on the level of small talk, business, politics or sports.

"Out of Bounds"

Really important matters that touch us personally, such as religious belief or personal conflicts and problems, are "out of bounds" in discussion. If brought into conversation, they are either ridiculed or frowned upon by those who themselves are often too frightened or threatened to enter into serious personal matters. And so these things are left for the psychiatrist, marriage counselor, attorney or clergyman.

Sharing the Lord

So it is that prayer-meetings have great appeal for those who want to meet others in a situation of equality as brothers and sisters before the Lord—to praise, share, read Scripture, sing lively songs, or even, if we are so inclined, just rest silently in the Lord among fellow-Christians.

Sharing Jesus with others in a personal way is a religious experience on the deepest level. In it the Holy Spirit works His wonders in each of us and in all together since together we are the Body of Christ. One comes to love the Body of Christ at prayer-meetings, to experience the joy and pain of the members of the Body. One learns the deepest meaning of "Church," the People of God united in Christ.

Helplessness

A second reason many attend prayer-meetings is their great sense of helplessness without Jesus Christ. This need can be manifested in different ways: an addiction, a compulsion, intellectual confusion, a bad marital situation, or just plain emptiness.

Least Likely To Attend

It seems to me that those least likely to attend prayer-meetings are those who are most satisfied with their spiritual life, or lack of it. It is only when one feels "broken" that he or she becomes hungry for the healing power of Jesus. Sometimes, though, God is the last one we are likely to turn to. In fact, many are unconsciously so angry with God that they are not able to turn to Him. These must first learn to "forgive" God for the "rotten deal" He has given them in life. Others, again, are not broken enough to see Him as their only real support.

Supreme Purpose

The purpose of attending prayer-meetings is not to solve personal problems. The supreme and indispensable purpose is to praise Jesus as Lord in a community setting. It should not surprise us that many benefits flow from such an eminent act of religion, since our highest spiritual activity and our best human interests are intertwined. In the past we did not think so. We believed that true prayer and love of God were made possible only by rejecting or denying what is human. We were afraid "lest having

Him we must have naught beside" (Francis Thompson).

Our Best Interests

We know now that the experience of being Christian is directly related to the best interests of a person as an individual and as he or she relates to others. For the Church is above all a community of believers. By oneself a person cannot continue to grow as a Christian. The Spirit of God came upon a community at Pentecost. We still receive the Spirit primarily through the Christian community, the Church, the People of God.

Christian Joy

It is no wonder, then, that Christians are finding great joy and satisfaction in attending their regular prayer-meetings. What else ought we expect from a combination of the power of the Holy Spirit, the special presence of Jesus to those "gathered in His Name," and the loving sharing of our lives on a serious and deep level? It is not at all surprising that many look forward eagerly to their weekly meetings, that the hours pass quickly at the meetings, and that people are reluctant to go home after several hours.

Others Love Jesus

I am not suggesting that there are not many other Christians for whom Jesus is the center of their lives. Indeed, He loves all people and comes to us in many ways. As I said above, He comes to us especially as a community. And within that community, the Church, He comes to us variously, especially through the Eucharist. What I am saying here is that the particular way of finding Christ that I have been describing has been disregarded by us for centuries. I am glad that I have found it. It is making a great deal of difference in my Christian life, as I know it is doing in the lives of many others.

New Emphasis on Community

No one can be a Christian all by himself or herself. Christianity is, before all else, a fellowship of loving believers. Over the centuries, however, this basic personal relationship in faith gave way to an intellectual and legalistic approach to Christ and others. Somehow and somewhere we lost our sense of Christian fellowship. We began to worship God individually and vertically. Our eyes (and hearts and minds) looked upward toward God and downward toward self. We lost contact with our brothers and sisters in Christian worship. We prayed "next" to our neighbors, but not really "with" them. Often we did not know their names, much less their fears, their anxieties, their yearning, like our own, to be known and loved. Personal prayer meant individual prayer, a matter between God and me. External manifestations of one's religious feeling belonged only to the "holy person" or to the eccentric.

Now once again we Christians are reaching out personally to fellow-believers, to share with them a common faith in Christ the Lord. Instead of my fellow-Christians being an "object" of my prayerful intentions, I have now the opportunity, if I wish, to share with them what my Lord means to me, to let them tell what Jesus means to them, to pray together with them, perhaps to sing, to lean a bit on their strength, and they a bit on mine, and both together on Christ's. Of all the "signs of the times," freely-formed communities of faith and prayer are probably the most significant for the future direction of the Church.

A More Meaningful Faith

Today's need for shared faith is due, in part, to the sense of loneliness and helplessness that has come over many of us who, until recently, tried to be good Christians by depending directly on God, the Sacraments and the fulfillment of the laws of the Church. Religiously we lived in our "private worlds." Catholics, it seemed, could share anything in life with others except their personal relationship to Christ. At most, one could "discuss" religion with another, and even this, along with politics, was considered a dangerous area, since these two easily became occasions for argumentation.

It is true that we have had the documents of Vatican II to study and rejoice in. And so we have done. But, meanwhile, religious attitudes and practices we were familiar with all our lives began to disappear one by one: the way we "went to Mass," popular devotions, Lenten practices, etc. Many of us have lost our sense of security and certainty. And we are confused. On the one hand we are glad that the Council has taken place; on the other hand, while much of our personal religious life has become dismantled, nothing appeared to help us to "build it up again," to renew it.

Now this is no longer true. All around us small communities of Christians are being formed, who are not only faithful and loyal to the teaching and authority of the Church, but who are finding a new way of entering into the practice of their faith that is personally meaningful, realistic and practical. Their distinctive characteristics are love and joy.

Support for One Another

I said above that no one can be a Christian all by himself or herself. True as this is, it is also true that no one can be a Christian without personal decision, faith, conviction, and solitary reflection and prayer. As is manifest in the life of Christ, true religious practice takes into account both its social and its individual aspects.

We live in a socially conscious age. We speak of, and we actually have, "one world." Today we are more conscious than ever before, it seems, of our human solidarity and of our mutual need for personal support.

Sign of Community

As our dependence on legal structures wanes, our need for personal support from one another increases; for we cannot live without support, one way or another. We are seeing ever more clearly that we cannot sustain and nourish our faith in today's world without the strength that comes from Christ through the community. We cannot be members of Christ apart from His Body, the community of believers.

A living community of Christians, then, does not come into being, as we might have thought in the past, by mandate from above. Neither does it simply "happen" of itself. Christian community is always in a dynamic process of growth, entailing all the sacrifice, tension and pain that is required in the development of any truly human family. The one great difference, however, between a Christian community and any other human society is the explicit recognition of Christ as Lord and of the action of His Spirit through the acceptance and use of the diversity of gifts of all the members of the community. The distinctive sign of this Christian dimension will be the manifestation of love for one another. Without this, St. Paul reminds us, all other gifts are sterile and meaningless.

6.
The Church and the Gifts

We said above that, in its essential structure, the Church is no less charismatic than it is hierarchical and sacramental. This is clearly evident when we look at the Church in its very beginnings, as manifested in the pages of the New Testament.

The First Christians

It was normal procedure for the first Christians to submit their deliberations and decisions to the Holy Spirit. The Acts of the Apostles is the account of an enterprise shared together by God and man. The Spirit was consulted, listened to, and followed in matters large and small, personal and communal.

Relationship with God was mediated by the gifts of the Spirit. These were given for individual growth in Christ (sanctifying gifts) and for the building up of the community (charismatic gifts). All the gifts together constituted a spiritual dynamism, empowering believers to accept and to live the Lordship of Christ in all aspects of daily life. The whole community of Christians (the Church) was nourished and fortified by the Sacraments, especially the Eucharist. Everything was ordered, under the Spirit, by those who had pastoral gifts of teaching and guiding the Body of Christ. This last is what we call today the hierarchical dimension of the Church.

Integration of Three

What we see then, in the New Testament, is an integration and balance of gifts, Sacraments and authority. The Church has been from its beginning charismatic, sacramental and hierarchical. The normal tensions that arise between these dimensions are tempered and used by the Holy Spirit to "build up the Body of Christ" (Eph. 4:12). Each dimension is essential; each enhances the meaning and effectiveness of the other two.

Gifts Recede

For a variety of reasons over the centuries, the gifts of the Spirit lost their centrality in Christian life, while Sacraments and authority became increasingly emphasized. The place of the individual with his or her distinctive gifts receded, except for outstanding Christians, the "Saints." The charismatic gifts of a Francis of Assisi or a Catherine of Siena were acceptable (although usually not in their lifetime). For the rest of us, personal holiness and distinctive gifts were an individual and private affair. Ultimately the ideal Christian became one who received the Sacraments and obeyed God through the Church. Individual gifts of the Holy Spirit, once normal and frequent, were considered extraordinary and rare.

Believers Create the Church

As to one's place in the membership of the Church, the hierarchical Church has long been interposed between God and the individual believer. The "Church" thus acted for, approved, disapproved of, guided and restrained the "ordinary" Christian. The corresponding virtues in the latter were docility and obedience. These were the supreme measure of the "good Catholic." Since Vatican II, however, the undeniable authority of the hierarchy is more and more seen and exercised as service rather than dominion.

With our growing acceptance of the active role of every baptized believer in the total life of the Church, we are gradually accepting, too, the "incarnational principle," namely, that all that is truly human is an access to the divine. Our present understanding of a human being is of one who grows into (becomes) himself or herself by means of his or her own responsible decisions. It sees him or her growing in the mastery of his or her own biological and physical life and environment. In the same way, and for these very reasons, contemporary theology sees a human being as the creator of the Church of the future. If the Church is persons (the People of God), then in creating himself or herself a believer creates the Church.

Our Share in the Kingdom

So it is that the "image and likeness of God" in us has taken on an added meaning. Not only is a human being intelligent and free like God, but he or she is also like Him in the use of intelligence and freedom. A human being, too, is a creator. Together with God he or she creates himself or herself, his or her world, the Church, and ultimately the Kingdom of God.

In willingly accepting the "burden" of creating the Church of the future the Christian really has no cause to be afraid, for he or she will know the "rest of soul" that Christ has promised to those who face up to the work of fashioning the future: "My yoke is sweet and My burden light." From the beginning the burden of suffering has been attached to the daily task of living and working. Christ, however, has transformed it into a source of joy.

We need not take this in any abstract, mystical sense. The joy that comes from work accomplished is a matter of common experience. In fact, there is nothing that gives us such deep contentment in our ordinary life as some creative activity, some task whose fruit we feel is ours alone. And there are few forms of suffering so keen as the monotony of inactivity.

What exhilarating experience awaits us Christians if we can learn to laugh at our ancient fears and begin to get on with the "burden" of our share in creating the Kingdom of God!

Renewal

Among other things, the Charismatic Renewal is calling attention again to the importance, in both the Church and the individual Christian, of the action and gifts of the Spirit. While spiritual gifts have never been lacking in the Church, their fundamental place in each person's life was all but lost. Had it not been for the well-known effort of Cardinal Suenens at the recent Council, the section on charismatic gifts in the Church (n. 12) might never have been written into the *Constitution on the Church*.

Complementary Gifts

As one attends prayer-meetings, he or she comes to appreciate more and more the abundant gifts of the Spirit to the People of God. He or she learns to value these gifts for their own precious sake, for the love he or she bears the Church and for his or her own personal growth. It is at once both humbling and encouraging to realize that God blesses even the most "ordinary" people with great and useful gifts that complement one another and "build up the Body of Christ." Their variety and distinctiveness make one love more dearly the Body of Christ, for whose benefit all the gifts are intended. Through them one enters into an experience of the Church at a very deep level, that of the unity and variety of the members of the Mystical Body of Christ.

7.
Baptism in the Spirit

When I first heard a Catholic say he had been "baptized in the Holy Spirit," it seemed to me that he was claiming for himself some special experience that was unrelated to the Catholic doctrine I had learned. Since then I have found out: (1) he was adding nothing to traditional Catholic teaching about Baptism, for "there is one Lord, one faith, one Baptism" (Eph. 4:5); (2) the phrase "Baptism in the Spirit" is scriptural; (3) the power of the Spirit received in Baptism and Confirmation is still waiting to be "released" in many Christians; (4) something special is happening to many in the Charismatic Renewal connected with "Baptism in the Spirit."

Transformation

Many who regularly attend prayer meetings undergo a transformation in their Christian lives. This change for the better takes place most often when a group prays together for the "release of the Spirit" in someone, usually with a "laying on of hands" during prayer. Theologian Kilian McDonnell, O.S.B., interprets it this way: "Baptism in the Holy Spirit manifests itself in an adult when by either a crisis act or a growth process he says 'yes' to what objectively took place during the rite of initiation" (Baptism and Confirmation).

Origin of Term

As I looked into the origin of the phrase, I found that Jesus Himself used it when He told His disciples: "In a few days you will be baptized with the Holy Spirit" (Acts 1:5). I also found that in each of the four Gospels John the Baptist states that it is Jesus who will baptize us in the Holy Spirit. Whatever, then, this "Baptism in the Spirit" may really be, there is no doubt that it exists, that according to John the Baptist it is one of the main reasons for Christ's coming among us, and that it is Jesus who baptizes us in the Spirit.

Not a New Sacrament

As to its connection with Baptism of water and Confirmation, theologians generally see "Baptism in the Spirit" as the realization and the experience of the effects of having received the Holy Spirit in these Sacraments. It is simply a "release" of the power of the Holy Spirit already within us.

Effects of Baptism in the Spirit

Whatever the theological explanation of this conversion, its effects are very evident in a growing number of Christians. I have known these effects in my own life, and still know them: a more intimate, more personal relationship with Jesus; a greater love for private prayer; a desire to pray with others, with great joy and peace in so doing; a greater love for Scripture and for the Eucharist; increasing love for the Father and the Spirit and Mary; a greater love for the priesthood and for the Church; a new and important dimension of relationship to other Christians, namely a felt unity with them in the Body of Christ.

Has Always Occurred

There are some who experience the conversion that we are calling "Baptism in the Spirit" when they are alone. This, of course, has occurred in the history of Christianity very frequently. In the lives of the Saints there are numerous accounts of these moments of special grace: e.g., St. Paul on the way to Damascus, the Roman Cornelius when visited by Peter (Acts 10), Ignatius Loyola lying wounded in bed, and many others.

New Birth

Whether this moment of grace occurs in community or when alone, it is a "new birth," marking a commitment to Jesus as Lord and Savior. It therefore implies new responsibility together with the infusion of newly-experienced grace and gifts of the Spirit. It signals a reconfirmed commitment to private prayer, to the Eucharist, to Scripture, to the Church, to the service of one's brothers and sisters. Far, then, from being only a sign of Christian election and distinction (which indeed it is), it is the beginning of a deeper and more meaningful way of Christian life. To many who experience "Baptism in the Spirit" it seems as though they had never really been Christian before.

8.
Healing

We All Seek Health

One of the surest ways to get attention (and make a dollar) is to offer some new way to improve one's health, mental or physical. The attraction is irresistible. For not only is it normal and good to desire and seek health; it is the first law of our being to strive to remain alive. No one in his right mind will not seek health and growth.

Consider the crowded waiting rooms of doctors' offices, physical therapy programs, psychotherapy, weight-reducing plans, natural food fads, etc. Human health and growth is behind the whole thrust of the medical profession. It ennobles nursing. It explains the Pure Foods Administration, ecology, and sanitariums.

"Raison d'être" of Church

On another level, human health and growth is the "raison d'être" of the Church, of the Sacraments and of the Incarnation itself. We recite each week in the Eucharistic Liturgy that Jesus Christ "for us men and for our salvation (spiritual and temporal health) came down from heaven." The very name of Jesus means "Savior." Savior from what? From all that weakens and destroys man's health on every level—in other words, from all the effects of sin.

Good News: New Life

Indeed, then, we are most truly human (and Christian) when we seek the welfare (health) of man (ourselves and others). This is the sum total of the Gospel, the "Good News" of Christ. "When we were baptized we went into the tomb with Him and joined Him in death, so that as Christ was raised from the dead, we too might live a new life" (Rom. 6:4). "Through His wounds you have been healed" (1 Pet. 2:24).

Here and Now

The whole thrust of Christianity is to heal. Christians are beginning to appreciate more and more that Christ's healing power, mentioned in every portion of the Gospels, is meant to come to us here and now and to make us healthy on every level of our being, spiritual, emotional and physical. Through the power of the Holy Spirit sent by Christ, we are witnessing on every side today God's gracious response to the beautiful Sequence of Pentecost Sunday: "Heal our wounds, our strength renew; on our dryness pour thy dew; wash the stains of guilt away." In this liturgical prayer we are asking for health on every level of our being. And the Spirit is generously responding today. God is "saving" His people in mind and body.

Jesus Is the Healer

While you or I, or Kathryn Kuhlman or Oral Roberts may pray for healing, it is only Jesus Christ who actually heals through us. His work of salvation in us is an ongoing process. There is never a moment when He is not healing every one of us from sin and its effects. Christ loves all men, died for all men, and wishes to save (heal) all men. This is the "universal salvific will of God" to which theologians have always referred.

We Cooperate

On our part, we can cooperate in healing and make it more effective in our lives. We do this especially through the Eucharist. The priest says before Holy Communion: "Lord, I eat Your Body and drink Your Blood. Let it not bring me condemnation, but health in mind and body." Everyone says: "Lord, say but the word and I shall be healed."

We also cooperate with Jesus in healing through the Sacraments of Reconciliation and of the Sick, through our prayers, through our love for one another, and in the many other ways in which we open ourselves to the power of Jesus in our lives.

Proper Context

The peace and joy of the Sacraments, the cures at Lourdes, and the healings that take place daily through prayer and the "laying on of hands" have one single inexhaustible source: Jesus Christ. He is the sole religious healer, whatever the time, the place, the manner of prayer for healing, and no matter who does the praying, "The Spirit (of Jesus) breathes where He will" (Jn. 3:8).

Praying for healing that is associated with the Charismatic Renewal is rightly judged only in this context of Christ's ever-present saving power in human life.

Gift of Healing

St. Paul tells us (1 Cor. 12:9) that some Christians have a special gift of healing from the Holy Spirit. This means simply that, by God's gift, Jesus heals more effectively through the prayer of some of us. This gift, however, is never separate from the love of Jesus for others and from our faith in His promise. "And if you have faith, everything you ask for in prayer, you will receive" (Mt. 21:22).

Catholics and Healing

While the Gospels and our Liturgy emphasize the central role of Christ's healing power in our daily lives, we Catholics find it difficult to pray for healing. This is not surprising. For we are part of an age which has come to believe that: (1) only that exists which can be measured and or analyzed; (2) education (understanding) solves all problems; and (3) if there is a God, He does not "interfere" with laws of nature.

Confusion

The clash of our Christian belief and this modern mind-set leaves many in great confusion about healing. Most Catholics, I dare say, accept physical healings at Lourdes. Yet at the same time we have differing opinions about whether Jesus saves us in this world or only in the next, whether His saving power reaches only our "soul" (where sin "resides") or also touches our emotions and our bodies, whether He intended His healing power and the power He gave his followers to be effective only for a short time (the Apostolic Age?) or for the duration of Christianity, and whether healings today are restricted to certain places like Lourdes and to certain persons (the Saints).

In this confusion, we find some Catholics who will not accept any healings, even those of Lourdes. Most of us, I suppose, are in between: we have not really made up our minds one way or the other about healing.

As for me, I have witnessed healings here and as far away as Nigeria: mostly inner healings (emotional and relational) but also some physical healings. I know it is basically a matter of my faith both in Jesus' power and in the testimony of those who claim to be healed. For me the "fruits of the Spirit" are quite manifest in these instances. I am content to leave it at that.

9.
Healing and Forgiveness

Forgiveness of others is the most essential preparation for the reception of God's healing. Christ's saving power follows upon our act of reconciling ourselves with our neighbors, especially with those who have hurt us. Jesus made it clear that forgiving others is a condition for being forgiven by the Father.

Often Ingrained

Our unwillingness to forgive others is often deeply ingrained in us. We are often most reluctant to acknowledge its presence, or, if acknowledged, to rid ourselves of it.

It is reported that Mark Twain once said: "I really don't hate anybody; but if ever I do, I already have a fellow picked out." In his humorous and subtle way he was pinpointing one of our most destructive inclinations: resentment, unwillingness to forgive. And he implies that sometimes we have no intention of forgiving certain people. In fact, we might even relish and enjoy our resentment, since we feel that it gives some justification to what we say and do.

Unchristian Attitudes

The fact is that there is no attitude that is so un-

Christian as unwillingness to forgive, and, by
Christ's own assertion, there is nothing that so surely
separates us from the love and forgiveness of the Father. "If you forgive others the wrongs they have
done you, your Father will also forgive you. But if
you do not forgive the wrongs of others, then your
Father in heaven will not forgive the wrongs you have
done" (Mt. 6:14-15). It's as simple as that!

It is also a fact that many of us who say daily:
"Forgive us our trespasses as we forgive those who
trespass against us," not only tolerate our inner
resentment, but even cultivate it. We can easily deceive ourselves in this matter. We can rationalize,
justify, defend and explain away this spiritual cancer
of unwillingness to forgive and to love.

There are many of us "religious" persons, out-
wardly engaged in the work of the Lord, whose
mind-set is negative, critical and unloving. In contrast, sometimes, to our smiling faces and perhaps
meek and inoffensive manner, rarely do kind and
loving words of encouragement and praise come from
our lips. We can provide every reason to justify our
critical approach, to illustrate how what others do
is "wrong." We find it hard to tolerate human error.
After all, are we not to strive for "perfection"?

Unfortunately, however, our negative judgment
usually involves the person who falls short of our
standards. We know that hating the sin and loving
the sinner is a Christian ideal; but how often in practice we fail to make the distinction!

Impedes Healing

No one of us is without resentment, which we

tend to suppress and/or rationalize. We simply do not recognize how greatly it impedes God's healing power within us. It is true that negative feelings of anger, of resentment, depression, disappointment, etc., are normal reactions. Moreover it is part of emotional growth to learn not to repress these feelings, but to recognize them for what they are, and to learn to accept and deal with them. (Christ Himself was angry on occasion, was disappointed by His disciples, and even saddened to tears by the death of Lazarus.)

It is one thing to acknowledge, accept and deal with negative feelings. It is quite another to foster resentment against the persons who have occasioned them. The latter attitude impedes both natural and supernatural growth.

Taking Stock

An effective way for us to realize how unforgiving we are is to call to mind persons who have been, or still are, part of our lives: parents, brothers, sisters, teachers, co-workers, neighbors, etc. As we think of those who we feel have hurt us in life, let us observe our present feelings in their regard. Are these feelings still negative? Do we still resent these persons? Do we still feel bitterness toward them?

Have we ever told Christ that we forgive them, that we want them to forgive us, that we love them and ask His blessing upon them? (At this point you may feel like saying to me: "Are you serious, Father? Look what they did to me!") If so, how Christian are we? And do we realize that this unwillingness to forgive and to love is the prime obstacle to God's healing power within us? Christ meant what He said about the severe punishment given to the unforgiving servant: "This is how My Father will treat you, if you do not forgive your brother, every one of you, from your heart" (Mt. 18:35). Do we wonder, then, that the peace of Christ fails to fill our hearts, when we are constantly blocking it out!

Forgiveness Builds Community

What I am saying here about unwillingness to forgive has much wider implications than its effects upon us individually. Its importance for building up the Christian community is essential. Christ made it clear that we are not prepared to approach the altar with our gift if we have not first set ourselves right with our neighbor. "So if you are about to offer your gift to God at the altar and there remember that your brother has anything against you, leave your gift there in front of the altar and go at once to make peace with your brother; then come back and offer your gift to God" (Mt. 5:23-24).

There can be no Christian community if there are no Christians, just as there cannot be Christians without the Christian community. The individual and the communal aspects of the Christian faith are each mutually necessary for the existence and growth of the other. Just as we cannot live in a Christian way without the continuous support of fellow Christians, so the Christian community itself depends greatly on what individual believers bring to it in faith and love.

Eucharist and Forgiveness

God does not work in and through us by bypassing our individual dispositions. This is true especially for our Eucharistic gatherings. Although the Eucharistic Assembly is the center, the culmination and the distinctive form of the Christian community, it does not in itself make us Christian. It is a gathering of those who are celebrating, nourishing and witnessing to what already exists among us, namely "one Lord, one faith, one Baptism." And, for the effectiveness of each particular Eucharistic gathering, sincere love of our neighbor without exception is presupposed. Otherwise why would Christ have us first go and be reconciled with our brothers and sisters?

Conversion Means "Letting Go"

Only a short time ago, with Vatican II, the People of God began their process of conversion. And while it cannot be doubted that a number of worthwhile and needed changes have already taken place in the Church, they are mostly external and procedural, and they are only in the process of being realized.

But the real struggle to make Vatican II a reality is being fought silently and unobserved within the souls of all of us who feel the conflict between the aims and ideals of the Council and the deeply embedded mind-sets and emotional habits of religious thought and action that were formed in us over many generations. We are still in the first phase of radical change. We are psychologically on the way down, and will probably be so for a time to come. We have yet to "hit bottom." When we have done so, then, please God, we will "find ourselves" again, "put it all together," and start back up the hill to become what Christians ought to be in this age.

We are still trying to "let go" of the encumbrances of the past that blocked our vision, tied us down, hindered our growth, gave us a false sense of security, or in any way shut us off from our brothers and sisters and, therefore, from true Christian discipleship. Even what we have relinquished up until now in religious practice and attitude is making us begin to feel the pain and terror that accompany loss of identity. For, religiously, many are at present not so sure of who they are or what they believe. The beautiful Bride of Christ is confused, uncertain, afraid, unattractive. It is a time when we need hope badly because, for many, the immediate future is mostly dark. Our strength is ebbing and we are a long way from home. We see little help coming from any direction.

We Acknowledge Our Mistakes

It is the age-old story of the Prodigal Son. How well Our Lord understood what it means to really change! How well He delineated the downward progression of anyone who surrenders true values for false ones! Some Catholics are at that point where the Prodigal almost "filled his belly with the husks that the swine did eat and no man gave unto him." Some of us are unfortunately doing just that. Some of us are turning elsewhere than to union with Christ and one another in love, and to reliance on the Spirit for the sustinence we presently need. As Christians nothing else will sustain us, for no matter how appealing, these substitutes are, by comparison, "husks for swine."

Like the Prodigal, too, we Catholics must now

begin to say to Our Father that "we have sinned."
Indeed there is much that we have to repent of both
individually and together. Mostly we have sinned
against the human person and so have offended God.
We have sinned against others by our overbearing
self-righteousness.

Call it triumphalism; call it exclusivism; whatever it was, it separated us from our brothers and sisters. Only we had the truth; only we knew the an-
swers. Only our Sacraments were holy. Only our
priests could bring men and women to God. Only our
causes were just throughout the centuries; all others
were either malicious or ignorant.

Finding the Way Home

We have sinned against ourselves and those en-
trusted to our care, and so have offended God. We
taught our children to war against their very selves—
to repress their feelings, chastise their bodies, control
their thoughts, despise their very existence on God's
good earth—and all this in the name of virtue. And
all the time, God help us, we were the ones who were
ignorant.

I am loath to think that many of us were malicious, although some few, of course, relished the
power that comes from control over other human
beings. There are few greater sins conceivable than
to manipulate, to use persons. Most of us were, and
perhaps still are, docile sheep. Some are refusing to
continue any longer in a condition of controlled
childhood and are severing their relationship with
the Church. This to me is a wrong solution, but it is
their decision, and I pray that they will find peace
and strength.

For those of us who want to find our way "back home," we must, like the Prodigal, recall the values once offered to us in Our Father's house. We must return to the Scriptures and recall how it was then. This is what is happening in the Church today. This is what the Fathers of the Council have told us to do. They have given us guidelines in the documents of Vatican II.

The Father Awaits Us

There is no question that repentance must become central in our attitude if we are to be really Christian again. When Christ and the Baptist first appeared in Judea, their message was: "Repent and do penance, for the Kingdom of God is at hand." Mostly, then, we Catholics, and indeed all Americans, must realize the need of repentance in our lives before we can take that first step back up the hill. We have to honestly acknowledge before God, before our brothers and sisters, and before ourselves, that we have sinned. We have to be ready to let the tears flow from our eyes and not be ashamed of them, but be ashamed of ourselves, before we can move along together back to God.

One thing is certain: we are not going back home alone. We left home alone perhaps and possibly that is the reason we left at all: because we were alone, because we never knew the strength and the grace and the joy of the love of Christ and one another without which Christianity has no meaning. Like the Prodigal, we are learning. We will never be alone again. When we do make our weary way back we can be sure we will see Our Father waiting for us, with arms outstretched, on the crest of the hill!

Year of Forgiveness

In the light of this, then, we can understand the tremendous significance of the recently completed Holy Year, a Year of Reconciliation. How beautiful! How appropriate! How filled with promise for the specific needs of men today! Unquestionably Christ through His Vicar is telling us that He stands ready to pour out His Spirit upon us, to "bend that stubborn heart and will; melt the frozen, warm the chill; guide the steps that go astray" (Sequence of Pentecost).

Begin Now

There is something you can do, dear reader, to begin to prepare yourself for the influx of the healing Power of the Spirit. You can begin by bringing a sense of reconciliation into your own heart. You can begin by forgiving anyone toward whom you presently feel bitterness—the one who makes you upset when you think of him (her), whom you refuse to phone, or write to, or talk to, or refuse to pray for (even though perhaps he or she has passed on), or upsets you when he (she) comes into your presence. If you think this is simple, just try making an act of love this very moment for the person you feel you least want to meet or talk to.

"Forgive" God, Too

And how about "forgiving" God for all the tough things in life that you think He could have made different for you? Many of us are angry toward God, but will not admit it to ourselves. How about telling God right now that you are grateful for every minute of your life?

Forgive Self

Finally, how about letting up on yourself and forgiving yourself for not being what you think you "ought" to be? Sometimes the last person we will forgive is ourselves. Give yourself a break! Forgive yourself. Say: "I'm glad I'm me. Thank you, Lord." I think this is where many of us have to start—with ourselves.

10.
Speaking in Tongues and Prophecy

Based on Faith

When one attends a prayer-meeting for the first time, speaking and singing in tongues seem very strange. It makes no sense that grown, intelligent people should be uttering sounds which they admit are unintelligible to themselves or to others. But, by the same norm of ordinary experience, it makes no sense that we should eat what looks and tastes like ordinary bread and call it the Body of Christ. It makes no sense, unless I accept it in faith. Then it makes a great deal of sense. In fact, the Host becomes for me a means of holy communion, even physical communion with Jesus Christ. And I treasure it dearly. So it is with the gift of speaking in tongues. I accept it in faith and I treasure it dearly.

One can no more be persuaded by logic alone to accept speaking in tongues than he or she can be persuaded by logic alone to accept the Eucharist. Here is what Scripture says about the first mention by Jesus of eating His Body: "He taught this doctrine in Capernaum, in the synagogue. After hearing it, some of His followers said: 'This is intolerable language. How could anyone accept it?' " (Jn. 6:59-60).

Contradicts Senses

The Eucharist and speaking in tongues are both gifts from God in the area of faith which contradict our senses. In his lovely hymn to the Eucharist "Adoro Te," St. Thomas Aquinas wrote: "Sight, touch and taste are deceived with respect to You (Jesus)." Just as the Eucharist deceives our eyes, hands and tongue, so does speaking in tongues deceive our ears. In both cases, things are not what they seem to be.

Gifts from God

It is not inappropriate to compare the Eucharist and speaking in tongues. The basis for both gifts is in Scripture and in the constant teaching of the Church. Of course, speaking in tongues is by no means as great a gift as the Eucharist, which is Jesus Himself physically present. In fact, St. Paul calls speaking in tongues the least of the gifts, although he boasts that he uses it more than anyone else. My point here is that they are both gifts from God for our spiritual good. We may not look down on any such gift.

Private Prayer

There are three uses of the gift of tongues that we know of. The most common use is for individual, private prayer. "Anybody with the gift of tongues speaks to God, but not to other people; because nobody understands him when he talks in the spirit about mysterious things" (1 Cor. 14:2). An increasing number of Catholics today use the gift of tongues to allow the Spirit to ask for the things we most need and which often we ourselves do not know. "In the same way the Spirit comes to help us, weak as we are. For we do now know how we ought to pray; the Spirit Himself pleads with God for us, in groans that words cannot express. And God, who sees into the hearts of men, knows what the thought of the Spirit is; because the Spirit pleads with God on behalf of His people and in accordance with His will" (Rom. 8:26).

Effects of Tongues

Those who use the gift of tongues say that it helps them greatly in times of spiritual dryness and when they are depressed or tired. It often produces a sense of the presence of God as well as joy and peace.

Praying with Others

The gift is sometimes employed when praying for another either individually or in a group. Again, at a prayer-meeting, those who have the gift may sing together "in the Spirit," as it is called. This prayer of praise generally issues in a beautiful harmony of all the voices.

Prophecy in Tongues

Another use of the gift of tongues, distinct from prayer, is mentioned at length by St. Paul in Chapter 14 of 1 Corinthians. He gives advice about speaking a prophecy in tongues. This occurs when someone speaks out (or sings) alone at a meeting. St. Paul advises that this use of the gift requires the presence at the meeting of someone who has the "gift of interpretation" which enables one to interpret what has been said in tongues for the upbuilding of the community.

Rare Use

The third (rare) use of the gift of tongues is to speak one language and to be understood in another. This is what happened on Pentecost when Peter spoke. Some saints have been known to have this gift.

Theological Statement

The recent "Statement of the Theological Basis of the Catholic Charismatic Renewal" (prepared by several theologians and finalized by Fr. Kilian McDonnell, O.S.B.) says about the gift of tongues: (1) "this charism, whose existence in the New Testament communities and in the early post-apostolic times is well attested, should not be given undue attention nor despised"; (2) the gift of tongues is "essentially a prayer gift enabling many using it to pray at a deeper level"; and (3) "those who stand outside the Renewal and attempt to evaluate the charism of tongues will fail if it is not understood in the framework of prayer."

Gift of Prophecy

At prayer-meetings frequently someone will speak out in the first person as though God the Father, or Jesus, were speaking. For some time I had trouble accepting this as a "word from God" (which is what "prophecy" here means). But now I accept it as a powerful way in which God speaks to us today. Not everyone has this gift. I do not. I know many who do have it, including some children. St. Paul writes: "Set your heart upon spiritual gifts—above all, the gift of prophecy" (1 Cor. 14:1).

Context

Prophecy must be understood in the total context of God's revelation to us. God is always speaking to us: in nature, through other men, and especially through His Son Jesus who is the "Word of God" among us. Christ revealed the Father's mind to us and still does so through the Church, through Scripture and through all the "People of God." Vatican II states: "The holy People of God share also in Christ's prophetic gift" (*Constitution on the Church*, n. 12).

Prophecy Always with Us

We are not accustomed to individuals speaking to us in God's name. But God has always sent prophets to influence, direct, console and chastise His people. Scripture presents many prophets, especially Jesus. The saints have often spoken God's word to us. What happens at prayer-meetings is not new.

True Prophecy

Naturally, not every utterance in the first person at a meeting is necessarily a word from God. It could be a pious statement or even a false prophecy. This possibility does not negate the fact that true prophecies are sometimes being spoken. The discernment of the community is called upon to judge prophecies. Norms of true prophecy are especially the fruits of the Spirit and right doctrine.

Receiving the Word

The Parable of the Sower makes us realize how

important are our dispositions in receiving the word of God, in whatever way it may come to us. In these confused times we surely need the word of God. We are deeply grateful that it is being spoken and heard at our prayer-meetings. It helps confirm our faith in Him as we hear Him speak in the Church, in Scripture and in so many other ways.

11.
Praise and Joy

Disappointed Child

Some years ago a niece of mine, then four years of age, came home from a party, face sticky with chocolate goodies, arms filled with presents and prizes. When asked how the party was, she replied: "No good." "Why?" I asked. "No soda," was her mournful reply. And so, the joy she might have felt because of all she had actually received was destroyed by the sadness of not having one more item!

We Deny Ourselves Joy

Similarly, the joy that might be ours in the acknowledgement and acceptance of the abundance of God's gifts is often overshadowed by anxiety and resentment about what we do not have. In prayer we tend to dwell constantly on our needs, rarely on our blessings. As a result we experience sadness, depression and discouragement, denying ourselves the joy that flows from the proper order of prayer that we learned in childhood.

Order of Prayer

Our prayer, we were taught, should be first adoration (praise) and thanksgiving; secondly, reparation (sorrow) and petition. We were given excellent models: the Our Father, the Hail Mary, the Psalms of David (which priests recite daily), and the beautiful Litanies of the Sacred Heart, of the Holy Name of Jesus, and of the Blessed Lady. Most important, we were given the Eucharist, which itself means Thanksgiving.

We Reversed Order

In our attitude and private prayers, however, this order was reversed. Prayer meant, above all, asking for something. Occasionally we expressed sorrow, especially before Confession, or if we thought we might die. Thanksgiving was a duty, particularly at meals. Adoration was something that angels did. Anyhow, it seemed to us that a perfect God has no need to be praised and thanked. In this we were right; it is we humans who have need to praise and thank God if we are to achieve some conscious relationship with a personal God. Interpersonal communication that is one-sided is a contradiction. "I am the Lord thy God" (Ps. 80:11) can never become a reality for us unless we acknowledge some of the ways in which He is the Lord our God. All creation provides us the means of acknowledging His dominion and goodness.

Grateful Heirs?

Besides, we Christians are the heirs to all creation. "In these days He has spoken to us by His Son, whom He hath appointed heir of all things, by whom also He made the world" (Heb. 1:2). "We are the sons of God. And if sons, heirs also; heirs indeed of God, and joint heirs with Christ" (Rom. 8:16-17). True as this is, it is reflected very little in our prayer. Rarely do we "count our blessings," that is, appreciate our inheritance. Instead, consciousness of our weakness and poverty makes prayer a burdensome task. Some simply stop praying.

More Than Pious Practice

Praising and thanking God is more than a pious practice; it is a duty, a privilege. It is also a constant source of joy. For it brings to mind all that is ours as co-heirs with Christ to all creation. Ours are the love of the Father and the gifts of the Spirit; the Sacraments and the Church; our human life; health, friends, sunshine, the breeze, the moon, a cup of tea; arthritis to help us know His suffering; a headache to teach us patience; the light in children's eyes; the dawn, the rain, etc.

So we believe; so we were taught. However, a basically negative view of ourselves and human life convinced us that holiness is much more a matter of ridding ourselves of our faults than an acknowledgement of God's greatness and mercy and abundant gifts.

Welcome Change

Recently, however, we are seeing a welcome change. Prayer of praise and thanksgiving is greatly on the increase today among Christians. One reason is modern man's more positive view of self and of things human, something that is reflected in all the documents of Vatican II.

Praise Produces Joy

The effects of habitual praise and thanksgiving to God in prayer are obvious and sometimes startling. The joy it produces sometimes seems unreal. It is not, however. It is simply the overflow of hearts and minds opened up to the sources of joy in life, namely, the abundance of God's gifts to us. In the daily, conscious acknowledgement before the Father of His countless gifts, what we do not have becomes relatively insignificant as we experience the joy Christ promised us. "Your heart shall rejoice; and your joy no man shall take from you" (Jn. 16:22). Christ really intended Christians to be joyful, but we block out that joy by destructive attitudes.

Psychological Basis

There is a solid psychological basis for the joy of those who engage daily in praising and thanking God. Explicit acknowledgement of God's goodness in every aspect of our lives gradually produces in us a sense of personal integration and wholeness. The fruit of this wholeness is joy.

Healthy People Praise

C.S. Lewis writes in his reflections on the Psalms: "I had not noticed how the humblest, and at the same time most balanced and capacious minds, praised most, while the cranks, misfits and malcontents praised least. The good critics found something to praise in many imperfect works; the bad ones continually narrowed the list of the books we might be allowed to read. The healthy and unaffected man, even if luxuriously brought up and widely experienced in good cookery, could praise a very modest meal; the dyspeptic and the snob found fault with all. Except where intolerably adverse circumstances interfere, praise almost seems to be inner health made audible."

As God's children, He has given us the universe as our "box of toys" to enjoy. But, like my little niece, we might narrow our vision down to one little thing and "miss the many-splendored thing."

12.
Learning To Pray

Communication

Everyone today realizes that interpersonal communication is the key to all meaningful human relationships. Where it breaks down, or is non-existent, there is little love expressed, little sympathy or understanding between persons. When we cease to communicate, then we fail to respond humanly to one another; we manipulate one another; we treat others as objects; we use them.

"Out of Touch" with Jesus

Considering this, it is sad that there are so many Christians who are completely, or almost completely, "out of touch" with Jesus Christ. It is sad because our relationship with Him grows or wanes in the same way that any human relationship does. He is a man. He loves us. He died for us. We need Him. He is for us "the Way, the Truth and the Life." No one comes to the Father except through Him. He stands ready to comfort us, strengthen us with His Spirit, guide us, heal us. And He is available to us. We who are Christian believe that He is present to us in a number of ways: As God He is everywhere. He is humanly present in the Eucharist, in a community of believers who acknowledge His presence, within us individually, in the word of God.

70

Attitude Toward Prayer

The strange paradox is that, while we acknowledge all of the above to be true, we still pay little or no attention to Him. In most of the important areas of our life He might as well be non-existent. Why is this so? Well, clearly it has to do with our attitude toward prayer. Now, even as I mention the word "prayer," our hearts sink. We have heard about prayer all our lives. We know we don't pray very well. We have tried often enough. Can anything I have to say here make any difference?

Jesus Refound

I don't know. I only know that I have finally learned how to communicate personally with Christ, and it is something I would not trade in for anything else in my life. I have at long last come to "know the man," and my life can never be the same. I am very grateful that, at this advanced stage of my life, I have this revitalized relationship to Jesus for whatever years remain to me. For I have no intention of "letting Him go"; I know He will never "let me go."

No New Formula

It is not that I have discovered some new formula for praying. I have heard nothing recently that I had not heard before. What did happen is that I finally came to really believe a few things I had long known and this has made the difference. Let me list four things:

Pray Your Own Way

1. No one can pray exactly as I do, because I am myself and no one else. Christ willingly accepts

my meager, distracted, confused, disordered, egotistical, "presentation" to Him. It's all I have! It's the best I can do! At last I am convinced that it is all He wants from me, precisely because it is the best I have. This has taught me to give Him each day the amount of time I decide upon and not cut it short, as I did in the past, because I felt I was not praying well. (I don't really spend very much time in prayer, but it is a great deal compared to the "nothing" I gave Him for years. And it adds up over the weeks and months. Most importantly, of course, it is changing my basic attitude toward life: more peace, more joy, less anxiety. Christ really does send His Spirit with special gifts, if we ask him.)

Learning Process

2. Prayer is a learning process. We only learn to pray by praying; there is no other way. Cardinal Newman once wrote that one learns to swim only by going into the water, not by reading all about swimming. I had spent so much of my life in trying to learn how to pray, by reading and thinking about it, and by "watching myself" while I was praying. Most often I gave myself a poor rating. Consequently, I was nearly always discouraged while I prayed, and I rarely prayed when I did not "have" to. Believing in prayer as I did, and leading others in prayer, I often felt hypocritical. There were years when only God's grace prevented me from throwing the whole thing up.

Thanks and Praise

3. When I am praying I spend most of the time

thanking and praising God for what He has given me, which is everything I have. St. Paul writes, "What have you that you have not received?" (1 Cor. 4:7). The answer, of course, is "nothing." Praising and thanking God takes my mind off my needs, reminds me of all the great things in life, provides an endless list of things to occupy my mind in prayer (the time goes by quickly this way), and brings a sense of joy after a while. Of course, I intertwine many petitions as they come to my mind. But mostly I tell Christ how great He is! What a difference it makes in prayer to get your mind off all the things you do not have, and to "count your blessings." After a while, what I do not have seems unimportant in the wider perspective of God's goodness.

Christ the Center

4. In all of this, what has happened to me is that Christ has become the center of my prayer, instead of myself and my needs. I am not surprised! He is not deceiving us when He says: "I am the Way," "No man comes to the Father except through Me," "Learn from Me," "I am the Good Shepherd," "If I be lifted up I will draw all things to Myself," etc. While turning to Christ, I still feel all the old guilt, inadequacy, distraction, etc., but it doesn't matter anymore. I believe I am doing the best I can. And He loves me the way I am.

No More Comparing

I suppose one way to sum up all this is to say that I have stopped comparing myself to others: saints in books, my fellow-priests, pious parishioners. (I really don't know how others pray, anyway.) They are probably looking at me and feeling inadequate. It doesn't matter now. As Paul said, "I am what I am by the grace of God" (1 Cor. 15:10).

Jesus—Lord of All

It is part of our Christian belief that Jesus is Lord of all. By His Death and Resurrection He gained dominion over all things. All creation rose in and with Christ on Easter morning. Further, our faith teaches us that the Resurrection is a dynamic, ongoing event and power in human life.

If it is not, what is the point of Christianity today? We believe that Christ is still wresting from the powers of evil their dominion over the physical world and all the affairs of men and women. This ownership and dominion He now shares with us. "All that the Father has belongs to Me" (Jn. 16:15). "You have received the spirit of adoption of sons whereby we cry Abba, Father—and if sons, heirs also, heirs indeed of God and joint heirs with Christ" (Rom. 7:15, 17).

Unfortunately we Christians are inclined to believe that the fruits of Christ's Life, Death and Resurrection are to be enjoyed by us only in the world to come. The truth is that Christ poured out His Spirit at Pentecost in order to enrich men and women in every succeeding age with the fruits of His victory. The Acts of the Apostles is a stirring account of the continuous and universal distribution of Christ's gifts to men and women, not the least of which is power and dominion over things created.

Christ's Presence Remains

For some reason Christians came to believe that

the manifestation of God's love and power through the instrumentality of people ended with the first or second century. There is nothing in Scripture to justify this belief. On the contrary, it is clear that Christ intended the fruits of His Resurrection to enrich all men and women in every age. One of the sad results of believing that the Christian's power over temporal things (for example, power to "heal sickness"—Mt. 4:23) was somehow terminated long ago is that the average Christian today has little appreciation of the power and action of the Holy Spirit that is currently benefiting many men and women through the love and solicitude of their brothers and sisters. This is truly a regrettable loss of a precious portion of our common inheritance with Christ.

More than anything else, the realization and experience of our co-ownership of the world with Christ produces joy! Only lately have I come to know this, for it is only recently that I began to claim the rights of my partnership with Christ. Like most of us, I suppose, for many years my attitude toward creation has been indistinguishable from that of non-Christians. For many summers I have been like any non-believer in my pursuit of a few hours, or days, at the seashore or lakeside. These things are, of course, still mine to enjoy, but they no longer constitute an experience separate from the joy of each day's appreciation of Christ's and my co-ownership of the whole world.

The joy of possessing something desirable is always a keen one, like a new house or automobile, or, for a child, a new bike, doll, or baseball glove. Is this not the reason for the indescribable joy of a child on Christmas morning when he or she catches sight of the presents under the tree? Poets and saints often enjoy this profound sense of ownership of the beauties of creation. St. Francis of Assisi felt kinship with everything living. Someone said of Shelley: "The universe is his box of toys."

Response of Praise and Joy

One might be tempted to think that any effort to come into greater conscious realization of our co-ownership with Christ of the human world would, in fact, lead us to unreality, would make "dreamers" out of us. Quite the opposite! It enables us to enter more deeply into mundane experience. Rather than fostering an elitist withdrawal from reality, it nourishes a realistic spirituality and motivates us to sincere involvement in the lives of people, the approach that Christ Himself adopted, exemplified and commanded us to follow.

What brings about the change in attitude that I have been describing? How can one acquire this great sense of joy? It is really a gift from God, but it is related to our own efforts. It is not especially difficult for one who believes in the Resurrection of Christ and in our union with Him through faith and Baptism. There is no secret, esoteric formula for the realization of one's Christian inheritance. It is simply a matter of putting into practice what we learned as children: namely, that adoration (praise) and thanksgiving toward God are our principal duties as rational creatures and as Christians.

Prayer—Openness to the Spirit

It is a question of learning to open up ourselves to God and His goodness by means of constant praise and thanksgiving for all His gifts to us. It must become a habit—what Paul described as "praying without ceasing" (1 Thes. 5:17). Unquestionably, great support for prayer of praise and thanksgiving is found in the various kinds of shared-prayer groups that are appearing among us. Through our growing sense of praise and thanksgiving to God for His gifts we gradually see and appreciate these gifts as our own, which, of course, they are.

Presently many Christians have no sense of joy about God's (and their) universe because they do not take prayer seriously. What power and joy await those who, by prayer, enter in the ever-present reality of Christ's Resurrection from the dead for the sake of us men and women!

13.
Emotions and Religion

Style of Piety

The style of piety of Catholics who attend prayer-meetings strikes some as too emotional, especially when first attending a meeting. It is true that there is a distinct emotional atmosphere which is not usually experienced by Catholics at religious gatherings.

The most frequently observed emotions are enthusiasm and joy. Frequently there is the physical accompaniment of hand-clapping and raising the arms.

A show of joy is sometimes suddenly and drastically followed by a period of almost absolute silence wherein the prevailing mood is one of peace, unity and the felt presence of God.

Not infrequently, too, an individual's prayer, petition for prayer, or witness to some blessing received will be uttered with overtones of gratitude and joy. Sometimes there may even be tears of joy.

What About Emotions?

What about emotions and religious practice? Why do Catholics generally have a distaste for physical expression at prayer? Why do we find it difficult even to raise our arms in prayer even when we are alone? We all know the answer.

Emotions and Reverence

It is the way we were brought up religiously. We have been taught that reverence for holy things and emotional expression do not go together. While some Protestant churches traditionally favored emotional expression in their meetings and praying, it is not the Catholic tradition, at least not in the last few centuries.

Norms for Reverence

Most of us remember well the norms given us as children for proper conduct in church or when at prayer: no unnecessary talking, especially no loud talking; no laughing, of course; singing could be joyful, but not too joyful. Surely no one spoke spontaneously from the pews at Mass or Benediction. Clapping hands was unheard of. "Dancing in the aisles" was as unthinkable as "going to the moon." We were taught that the ideal physical posture before God was kneeling, with eyes cast down and folded hands. In this way it was impressed upon us that our bodies were to be engaged as little as possible in religious expression. We priests recall the rubrics concerning our gestures and the use of the voice when we said Mass. These rubrics bound us in conscience. That is, their deliberate disregard could be either venially or even mortally sinful. Precision was the ideal. This ruled out individuality and emotional expression.

People of Our Times

It is not my intention to downgrade the past. We were all people of our times. Our external religious expression was very much in accord both with our view of faith and with the way we saw ourselves before God. Faith was primarily an intellectual act: the acceptance of truth on God's authority. Our concept of ourselves before God was principally negative: unworthiness, guilt, self-depreciation. This, in turn, was based on a dualist view of man, inherited from Plato. In spite of Catholic teaching to the contrary, it came down to us through the centuries in our asceticism, through Manichaeism, Catharism, Puritanism and Jansenism. In this view, soul and body are distinct entities. The soul is good and the body is evil. We older Catholics have only to recall our early training in spirituality to verify this.

Reaction to Past

There is today a strong reaction to the former repression of bodily and emotional expression. As a consequence, we see today in society widespread and exaggerated assertiveness of physical and emotional powers (witness the Rock scene). Nevertheless, the psychosomatic unity of man, and its importance, is becoming increasingly clear to us. Medicine continually verifies that human health depends greatly upon a proper balance between physical and spiritual powers.

Praising Totally

Religiously, too, we are learning to render to God greater glory for the vast beauty of His physical world. More importantly, we are learning to praise Him for and with our entire being, physical and spiritual. We are realizing ever more that we are neither angels nor beasts; we are human. This is our glory.

We can do nothing that is entirely physical, and nothing that is exclusively spiritual.

Greater Freedom

Many changes in the Liturgy are designed to allow for our greater participation not only in terms of the number of participants, age, and sex, but also in terms of greater involvement of the total person, body and spirit. Where there was strict conformity in the Liturgy in the past with reference to choice of text, manner of expression and physical stance, today there is a considerable measure of freedom to employ personal talent, creativity, and even spontaneity. Nevertheless, most of us still find it hard to "be ourselves" in expressing ourselves religiously. We ought all be sensitive to this in others. Sometimes we can be cruel in insisting that others participate in religious exercises for which they have neither feeling nor preparation.

Joy and Peace

As we begin now to participate more humanly, as individual persons and as members of the Christian community, in the expression of our religious beliefs, we are finding a wonderful thing happening all around us. An increasing number of Catholics are experiencing the joy of sharing their love of Christ. For the first time in their lives some are experiencing what it means to be Christian. They are tasting some of the peace and joy that Christ promised and which we were always taught was the rightful fruit of being Christian. "Peace I leave with you, My peace I give to you; not as the world gives do I give to you" (Jn. 14:27). "These things I have spoken to you that My joy may be in you, and that your joy may be made full" (Jn. 15:11).

Every day more Christians are learning to give physical and vocal expression to a new-found joy and love in their hearts. They are growing in the experience of the real freedom of the children of God!

14.
Eucharistic Celebration

Human Event

If some of us, with our current mentality, had been present at the Last Supper, we probably would have felt ill-at-ease at what went on. It was so unorganized and spontaneous! There was Christ suddenly washing the Apostles' feet; Peter arguing with Him about it; Judas suddenly leaving; John leaning against Christ's shoulder; several interrupting with "Is it I, Lord?"—and all that singing! The occasion for the institution of the Eucharist was not a very orderly event, but it was certainly a very human one.

Loss and Renewal

Somehow, over the centuries, the form of the Eucharistic Liturgy lost its spontaneity and human quality. Thank God, we are at present regaining some of the warmth and "down-to-earth" atmosphere that prevailed at the Last Supper. As slow, imperfect, and sometimes annoying as our liturgical renewal is, its basic direction is right and good.

"Sacraments for Men"

In the seminary we priests were often reminded that "Sacraments exist for men" and not men for the Sacraments. This meant that persons come first; that the Sacraments are means to an end, which is man's spiritual welfare; that we ought never put liturgical form and concern for reverence before the spiritual good of humans. The traditional motto "salus animarum suprema lex" ("the salvation of souls is the supreme law") states this principle very well.

Reverence Takes Over

But, unfortunately, our sacramental training and practice did not really follow this principle. Concern for reverence was the "supreme law," especially with respect to the Eucharist. Although we spoke constantly about the love of the Eucharistic Christ for us, and about our love for Him, in practice it was not love that prevailed, but fear of being disrespectful or irreverent. Our greatest concern was not to do something "wrong." There was a "right" way to hold one's hands, direct one's eyes, swallow the host, etc. Fasting was from midnight to the minute. And there were similarly precise rules for Penance and the other Sacraments.

With this background, then, some of us are understandably ill-at-ease with today's more human, natural and spontaneous approach to the Sacraments. Nevertheless, it is in accord with the atmosphere of the Last Supper and with the traditional teaching of the Church.

A Celebration

The Church has always taught that the Eucharist is meant to be a celebration of and by believers. Is it not the memorial of the saving Death and glorious Resurrection of Christ and of our participation in His victory? There is plenty of reason here for joy and celebration! In spite of this, our devotional

training and practice made us almost exclusively
conscious of the awful Death of Christ for us, sacra-
mentally represented for us miserable sinners. The
only admissible response on our part was sustained
and concentrated reverence. Any lapse or deliberate
"distraction" was irreverent, perhaps sinful. Individuality on or near the altar was a sign of lack of respect. The last one you were permitted to be was
yourself.

Historical Differences

Christian fellowship is one area where our Protestant friends can teach us a great deal. As we open
our minds and our hearts to these fellow-believers in
Christ, we are finding that they do many things as
Christians much better than we do. Not least among
these is their mutual sharing of religious experience,
witness and celebration.

The contrast between us in our basic religious
attitude is especially noticeable in our respective
church services. To Protestants the individuals attending were (and are) most important; to Catholics
the Mass itself is most important. It is of course, a
matter of emphasis. But it is clear that for Protestants people are important to God; for Catholics
God is important for people.

Not only do we differ in this basic emphasis,
but we Catholics used to turn every aspect of the difference into a claim for superiority or greater ortho-
doxy on our part. This is not surprising, for it becomes ever more apparent how arrogant we
Catholics have been for centuries toward anyone not
of our exact persuasion. Hans Küng writes: "For
many centuries we had no desire to know them (our

fellow Christians); or, if we did, it was only a desire
to know them from the worst side so that we could
at once defeat and dispose of them with theological
argument" (*Concilium*, Vol. 14, p. 1).

One thing that was an object of particular dis-
dain by Catholics was the Protestant's spirit of
Christian fellowship, caricatured by us in the image
of a clergyman shaking hands with his parishioners
after services. We saw it sometimes as a substitute
for the "real thing" that we had. After all, if you are
living in "invincible ignorance" and "religious
error," you have to do something. So while we concentrated on the Real Presence, Protestants had only
one another to depend on. Surely Christ was never
present in the practices of "false" religions.

We used to say that Protestant services were little more than "social gatherings." We would pride
ourselves on our more "divine" approach. Since we
"had the truth" we presumed that we could tran-
scend the merely human aspects of our faith. The
practice of our faith, we felt, had nothing to do with
that "secular" kind of community that they resorted
to. Besides we Catholics "had" communities, and we
still "have" them: religious communities of brothers,
sisters, and priests.

Sense of Community Missing

The ordinary parishioner has nothing to do with
religious community. A parish is not a community,
but a territorial arrangement of those who attend
Mass there and support the church and school.
Beyond that very few parishioners have much else to
do with a parish, except for an occasional meeting.

We "attended" Mass. We listened, watched and

said the private prayers of our choice while the priest took care of the Mass. Our obligation was to be "present." It was not important that we knew anyone else who was at Mass with us. The important thing was the Sacrifice, the truth of Christ's Presence on the altar, of His being offered and consumed. In fact, we all knew we had to be "present" for these three "parts" of the Mass. What we did in church was really secondary.

We said that it was a good thing that the Mass was said in Latin, because, no matter where we went in the world, we would find the identical Mass. This was true. It was also true, as a cynical friend of mine remarked recently, that we were treated the same wherever we went to Mass: we were ignored.

Liturgical Renewal

The new Liturgy was intended to change all this. Based as it is upon the concept of the Church as the People of God, and on the universal priesthood of all the baptized, it gave us high hopes for something that in most places just has not taken place. While we accept again the primacy of love of neighbor in Christian life, we are so inured to non-participation that we find it very difficult to reach out to others in matters of personal faith. A strange paradox becomes clearer: Catholics are one in belief and separated in practice; Protestants are less united in belief but somehow joined together in practice.

Most Catholics acknowledge that Vatican II initiated a "new spirit" of religious fellowship, but we do not encounter it often enough in our lives. The new Eucharistic Liturgy has been received indifferently. Occasional folk Masses and special liturgies enthuse us. For the most part the spirit of Vatican II has had little impact on our lives.

Christian Outreach

But there are signs that this is changing. We are beginning to reach out to others as fellow-Christians in a personal way, as St. Paul suggested: in song, in joy, in "bearing one another's burdens." We are starting to learn that our common faith can explicitly accompany any aspect of our life. It is not something just between me and God, between him or her and God. We really can be a community of believers if only we are not afraid to reach out in love to one another, to open up to one another. And the experience of this can change our lives, which is what, finally, Christianity has been all about since Judea and Galilee.

It is my belief that it is precisely the manifest experience of Christian love that is distinctive about a cursillo, or a priests' team-retreat, or a Christian "Awakening," such as take place all year round at St. Paul's Center in Brooklyn, N.Y. I am convinced that this is the only adequate explanation of the powerfully positive reactions of those who attend them.

There are many little posters, sayings and poems hanging on the walls of the halls and rooms at St. Paul's. When I was there recently one of them especially struck my fancy. It seemed to sum up for me the beautiful spirit of Christian fellowship that prevails there by the grace of God. I think it is by Camus: "Don't walk ahead of me—I may not follow. Don't walk behind me—I may not lead. Walk beside me—and be my friend."

Joy Again

Now, at last, the Eucharist is again becoming a joyous event, especially when believers bring to the celebration an existing bond among themselves of Christian faith and love. So, too, with the other Sacraments. They are becoming happy, human, loving events: real celebrations.

Christ's Multiple Presence

The attitude we have toward the Sacraments as celebrations tells each of us something about our understanding and appreciation of Christ's multiple presence among people. In the past we mostly limited His Presence (and action) to the Sacraments, especially the Eucharist. Although theology spoke of His presence in the whole Church which is His Body, as well as His Presence in the Word, in every community gathered in His Name, and in each of us individually, we were not ordinarily accustomed to respond to His many presences, but only to the Eucharist, the "Real Presence." Vatican II has brought back to our attention the traditional teaching about the many ways that Christ is present among men. I believe that the current revival of living faith in Christ is very much related to our growing appreciation of the ubiquitous presence and activity of His Spirit.

Community

For Christ is primarily present in and among humans, individually and in community. He is present in the Eucharist and in the Word of God only in order to increase His Presence and action within men. This is the unity Christ prayed for so earnestly at the Last Supper. He put His Body and Blood into people's hands to take and consume as a means to this unity.

More Human

His presence within us is not intended to destroy our humanity, but to make us more human, more like Him, and more like our own true selves. Clearly He accepts the human nature He wishes to abide in, with all its weakness and potential for error and for lack of respect. Do we not say that to err is human? And do we not add that to forgive is divine? Can we doubt for a moment that Christ understands and accepts our sincere and loving, but oh so human, approach to the Sacrament of His love?

Christ and Men United

There has always been in the Church, to the detriment of believers, the tendency to separate Christ from men, whether by looking upon Him as someone other than fully human, or by considering our humanity somehow unworthy of contact and union with Him. God became man in Christ precisely to unite all men to God through His humanity. In turn, the Sacraments were instituted to draw men to Christ. Anything, then, that tends to separate us from Christ in our common humanity is un-Christian and harmful, no matter how much it is proposed in the name of reverence for holy things. Christ is not a holy thing. He was (and is) a man among men. I am sure that He felt "right at home" at the very human supper table the night before He died. He is no less a part of all the local liturgies we sincerely, but sometimes so awkwardly, put together.

15.
Power of People
of God

Power of God

In the Charismatic Renewal one often hears references to the power of God in human life. The radical changes that are taking place in the lives of many, often giving order and commitment where before there was confusion and lack of direction, are clear evidence of the power of God among His People. Some theological reflections on the power of God among us will be helpful.

Church Born in Power

The Church of Christ was born in power. Jesus promised His disciples: "You will receive power when the Holy Spirit comes upon you" (Acts 1:8). And so it was on the first Pentecost. The body of believers received the Holy Spirit to enable them to continue His work among men.

Where Is It Today?

Since the power of Christ in His Church was not intended by Him to be limited to the Apostolic Age, what and where is this power in our Christian lives today? This is a question which the Charismatic Renewal is, willy-nilly, bringing into focus for all of us today.

We know that Christ died for all people and that His saving grace touches all. Our concern here is: How does the power of Jesus come to us in the Church?

Sacraments, Hierarchy, Gifts

I believe that the power of Jesus in the Church comes to the members of His Body through the Sacraments, the hierarchy and the use of the individual gifts of the Spirit. Without any one of these three "channels," Christ's Body is not what He intended it to be, for without sacraments the Body of Christ is devitalized, without authority it is disordered, and without the use of the gifts of its members it is rigid and immobilized. There have been periods in history when each one of these three conditions prevailed.

Where Do We See It?

How, then, do we see the power of Jesus working in the Church today? Do we see it only in the hierarchy? only in the Sacraments and hierarchy? only in individual gifts? in gifts and Sacraments only? Or in the three together? Surely, the Committee of Bishops on the Renewal saw it this way when, in January 1975, they encouraged priests to become involved in the Renewal so that it might be "integrated into the total life of the Church" where it clearly belongs.

We Catholics know well the sacramental and hierarchical relationship to the power of Jesus in our lives. What we are not familiar with is the power that we members of His Body have in relation to one another. Let me give an example of what I mean.

Small Group

Six of us sat around in a small circle. Three of

the six had traveled for two hours just to pray with us. For almost an hour we prayed together, reading Scripture, quietly singing some hymns, lapsing at times into the silence of peaceful unity in Christ. We "laid hands" upon the three as we prayed for their special needs. The love among us, the peace and joy, plus a tear or two, added up to a beautiful and moving experience. Jesus was clearly among us. And until that occasion we had never met before in our lives! Such is the power of the People of God.

Reservoir of Power

Week after week, month after month, as I sit down with my fellow Christians in groups large and small, I become increasingly convinced that we Christians together constitute a vast reservoir of spiritual power. This power is ready to be released in love, unity, joy and strength, whenever we "gather in His Name" and, through united prayer in expectant faith, open the channels of that power from Christ through the action of the Spirit.

Always Available

The power of the People of God is available at any moment, in any place, to any number of Christians who "gather in His name." It is my experience that He never fails to make His presence felt in the way that is appropriate to His living Body. He effects a sense of unity among us that is almost palpable; He produces in the Body a sense of peace that causes people to shut their eyes and rest in that peace. He brings about a sense of ease and comfort in the presence of others that makes one oblivious to time passing.

Living Body

What I am saying is that the Body of Christ is coming alive in its members. We are experiencing the great effects we have always believed come to us through Baptism, Confirmation, and especially through the Eucharist, namely, peace, unity, joy and strength. The reason for this is that we are now relating to one another in Christ as distinctive members of a living Body, unified by the same Spirit under the headship of Jesus. This is no longer just a doctrine; it is becoming a reality.

Not So in Past

In the past it was not so. Religiously we all did the same thing in the same way with no acknowledgement or use of the individual graces and gifts of the members of the Body. We prayed together in a single, predetermined, undeviating way. In those days the last thing one could be when we prayed together was oneself.

Christian Dignity

Now as we come together with our different gifts and talents from God, there is a sense of personal Christian dignity, a pride, a joy in the realization of one's uniqueness before the Father, intimacy with the Son, and openness to the action of the Spirit.

No Man an Island

Christian community is the key to this. For, just as we grow to maturity and "come alive" humanly in the bosom and by the support of our natural family, so also we "come alive" and grow to maturity as

Christian within the family of the People of God, the community of believers, the Church. But in this, just as in our natural family, growth is dependent on daily communication, understanding and sharing of oneself in areas that are important and personal. No one is an island, as a human or as a Christian.

The Spirit Builds Up
the Body of Christ

We may tend to universalize our limited experience, our personal response and our individual point of view. For example, God is graciously granting us tangible evidence of His Presence and work today in a number of Christian movements. The enthusiasm of those involved in them is justifiable and admirable. To desire to share our blessings with others is a normal, generous and worthy sentiment.

Sometimes, however, our very enthusiasm and zeal may cause us to lose sight of the larger perspective of the work of the Holy Spirit in the total Body of Christ, the Church. Every effective program for Christian growth is primarily the work of the Holy Spirit. "All these are the work of one and the same Spirit, who distributes different gifts to different people just as He chooses" (1 Cor. 12:11).

In our real concern for others, then, and even in our sincere gratitude to God for what He has done for us in a particular way, we may lose sight of the fact that the Spirit is at work in different ways in the whole Church. We may temporarily forget that freedom of choice and variety of invitation are essential in the Spirit's gentle call and in our response to it, as the text above makes clear. We must be careful, therefore, not to give the impression that the Holy

Spirit is at work almost exclusively (or, at least, most effectively) in the particular group or program with which we are associated, no matter what claim it may make to spiritual excellence and despite whatever excellent fruits it may have produced.

Charismatic Renwal—
An Instrument of Growth

.Personally, I am involved in the Charismatic Renewal. I see the Holy Spirit operative and effective in this growing movement. This is not to say that every prayer group is equally responsive and submissive to the direction of the Spirit, or that there is not great need in it for qualified and proper spiritual and theological guidance, especially by priests (who are eagerly asked to participate for this very reason), or that those who attend prayer meetings do not manifest the same weaknesses, ignorance, uncertainty and needs as do other Christians, or, finally, that the Charismatic Renewal does not have its share of enthusiasts who tend to repel others in their efforts to attract them.

Further, like any movement within the Church, the Charismatic Renewal is not an end in itself. It is an instrument for growth in the hands of the Holy Spirit. Its basic reason for existence is to help build up the Body of Christ by assisting Christians to submit more readily in their total lives to the action of the Holy Spirit. I find this happening in the particular prayerful and loving prayer group community to which God has graciously called me.

Varied Gifts Build Up the Church

We should never forget that, no matter how

generously God has dealt with us within a particular Christian framework, the Spirit "distributes different gifts to different people just as He chooses." There are countless ways that the Spirit builds up the Body of Christ. He works through and in a vast variety of Christian "gatherings." We have Christ's promise that "wherever two or three are gathered in My name, there am I in the midst of them" (Mt. 18:20). The Spirit works through our loving dialogue, but He is not constrained or limited by it. He works through meaningful and joyous liturgical forms, but these do not define the boundaries of His operation. The Spirit is present in our Christian concern for the poor, but social work is not the boundary of His effectiveness.

It is not fundamentally important what each "gathering" of Christians calls itself, or what technique each uses. The "one thing necessary" is that we be open to the promptings of the Spirit and docile to His leadership. For only the Spirit can fashion a Christian community; only He can build up the Body of Christ. The Power of the Spirit was present at the birth of the Church on Pentecost. His is still the Power and the Presence wherever the Church is being truly renewed today!

16.
The Priest and the Charismatic Renewal

"Grass-Roots" Movements

The Catholic Charismatic Renewal is a "grass-roots" movement. For the last decade prayer-groups have sprung up simultaneously in the most far-flung areas of the world. The beginning of the Renewal in time is usually attributed to those groups which appeared in Pittsburgh and at Notre Dame University and at Ann Arbor. But there is no causal connection between them and the proliferation of groups elsewhere. Clearly the Holy Spirit is working directly in the People of God everywhere. This is what I mean by a "grass-roots movement. In religious matters, especially of a doctrinal and devotional nature, the impetus and direction in the past has first come from ecclesiastical authority. This has not always been so in Church history, but it has been so in recent times.

Common Christian Bond

Because the Renewal is coming from the totality of the Body of Christ, the People of God, involvement in this style of piety on the part of bishops, priests and laymen and women alike has been, in the first instance, on the basis of our common Christian bond: our acceptance of Jesus as Lord and Savior.

This is in accord with the purpose of charismatic prayer-gatherings: to praise Jesus as Lord through the sharing of individual gifts for the "building up of the Body of Christ" (Eph. 4:12).

Brothers and Sisters in Christ

The principal requirement for this is to be able to relate to one another as brothers and sisters in Christ. In so doing, we do not detract from what each of us is in the manifold aspects of life (male, female, married, priest, young, old, educated, simple, etc.). On the contrary, this fundamental relationship to Christ and to one another fosters genuine Christian acceptance and enhances each person in the totality of our particular life and calling.

Hard for Many Priests

It is understandable that this kind of Christian equality in action can be difficult for many priests to enter into and accept. In our education and experience we are accustomed, not to equality with laymen and women in doctrinal and devotional areas, but to leadership and the use of authority. To see others take the lead, especially in our presence and without reference to us, can strike some of us as presumptuous and dangerous, even threatening.

In view of this, the following reflections on the relationship of a priest to a Catholic charismatic prayer-group may be helpful:

Shares Gifts

1. A priest's principal purpose in becoming involved in a prayer-group should be to share his personal gifts from the Spirit equally with all other

Christians present in a spontaneous and free manner. If he has any other principal reason for coming, he is not truly involved, no matter how praiseworthy be that reason.

Openness

2. As with other Christians, there is no area of his life from which he may not draw, under the guidance of the Spirit and the discernment of the community, whatever he feels is "profitable" for the up-building of the Body of Christ.

Leadership

3. He has no claim to a position of authority, or of leadership, in a prayer community solely because he is a priest. On the other hand, the fact that he is a priest should not be, in itself, a deterrent or a hindrance in the use of the gift of leadership, if he has that gift.

Teaching

4. A priest should not insist on teaching in a prayer-group solely because he is a priest. Nevertheless, he ought to make available to the group the wealth of his background and experience as a Christian teacher if, in fact, this exists. On the other hand, a prayer-group ought to expect such competence in a priest and make use of it where it exists.

Priestly Ministry

5. Since we are speaking here of Catholic groups concerned primarily with spiritual matters, to the extent that his priestly powers and ministrations fit into the over-all workings of the group, and espe-

cially when he is asked to do so, a priest ought to make them available to the community.

Likewise, a prayer-group should not disregard the spiritual benefits which complement the action of the Spirit in prayer-groups and which are available through the presence of a priest in their midst. I am referring here especially to the Sacraments of the Eucharist, Reconciliation and the Sick.

Concern for Doctrine

6. Because he is commissioned to teach and preach the Good News in union with the bishop of the diocese, a priest, especially when he is part of a prayer-group, must have a reasonable concern for the religious doctrine he encounters. He should avoid the extremes of a "watchdog" mentality on the one hand, and a lack of concern on the other. In turn, the prayer-group ought to turn to him for his expert guidance where it seems necessary and/or helpful.

Parish Priest

7. Since a parish priest must have concern for the total parish, if he is involved himself in a group, or if the group meets in his parish, he ought to have special concern for the integration of this group into the total life of the parish. Further, every priest who attends prayer-meetings should try to rectify anything that causes division from one's fellow human beings or in any way opposes the sacramental or hierarchical structure of Christ's Church.

17.
The Future of the
Charismatic Renewal

The Church's Renewed Witness

At first it seems futile and presumptuous to be concerned about what the Church will be like in the future. After all, Christ loves His Church. He not only promised to be with it "all days," but He sent the Holy Spirit to abide with it, to protect, guide and love it. One is tempted, therefore, simply to wait and see what God will bring out of the current profound changes in Christianity.

On the other hand, we also know that, by the mystery of the cooperation of grace and freedom, the Church of the future will be whatever we individual Christians create. So it is, then, that a realistic love of the Church impels us to be actively concerned about its future. And indeed many Christians are deeply concerned.

In one sense the Church is unchangeable; in another sense it must always change with the times. It is unchangeable in that it will always be comprised of those who accept the Lordship of Christ in faith, encounter Him in and through the Sacraments, and exercise their gifts and ministries variously to build up the Body of Christ and the Kingdom of God. The Church is changeable in that it must witness to Christ, saving and serving men and women in ways that are comprehensible in each succeeding age.

It seems to me that if we are judging the "signs of the times" rightly, two important features of the Church in the age we are entering will be personalism and pluralism. Although these are already being manifested in almost every area of Christian concern today, they are coming to our attention most dramatically and effectively in the recent appearance of a number of freely-formed communities of faith among us.

Signs of the Spirit

These Christian groups are prospering, it seems to me, precisely because of personal faith and initiative, spontaneity, and the diverse gifts that each Christian brings to the community. Among such freely-formed communities are the Charismatic Renewal, marriage encounter groups, Cursillos, Christian Awakenings, prayer groups, and Bible study groups.

The Church is undergoing radical revision in its self-understanding. I have tried, however inadequately, to spell this out. Disturbing and confusing as change may be, we ought never to forget that it is Christ in whom we finally find our rest. "Abide in My Love" is His invitation to us. Let us have eternal gratitude to the Father for sending us His Christ, who is the same yesterday, today and forever!

It is my belief that the Holy Spirit is manifestly at work in all of these new groups. They seem to bring to the fore the very qualities which I believe will mark most Christians in years to come: deep personal love of Christ, reliance on the Holy Spirit, a desire to share one's faith, love and prayer with other Christians, conviction, spontaneity, and joy. In this there is indeed a recognizable return to the style and spirit of early Christianity.

History has a way of repeating itself, it is said. Surely the action of the Holy Spirit cannot be tied to one age. Today, as I said, He is evidently at work in the Church. In many respects we are returning to what the Church was in its beginnings. We know that this is true in a theological, a biblical and a liturgical sense. Vatican Council II itself is prime testimony to this. But more recently we are seeing that this is true also in personal and social ways.

A Voice in the Wilderness

We are now coming to the end of the Church's "Middle Ages," the period of its cultural, political and religious ascendency, at least in the West. We are now entering into what Karl Rahner calls a "diaspora," that is, a time when the Church will indeed exist everywhere in the world, but as a minority, numerically, culturally and religiously. With the process of secularization this change has in fact been taking place for a long time. In time to come the Christian voice will no longer be the prevailing one, as it has been for centuries. In a pluralistic world it will have to contend again for attention in the market-place as it did in its first centuries.

Those who identify the Church only with its organizational structure and with acceptance and prestige before the world will see this change only negatively. To them it means only loss for the Church. Those who view Christianity primarily as personal commitment to Christ and to others will see the "diaspora" of the Church as a gain. Rahner views it theologically as a "must" in the sense in which

Christ said that scandal and "the poor" are always with us. They are situations that have to be faced and contended with. They are facts of life with which Christians must come to terms. We should not waste the energy bewailing them which might better be used in trying to eliminate them; nor should we, with "ghetto" mentality, withdraw and act as though they did not exist.

A Community of Believers

There will probably be very few, if any, "nominal" Christians in the future. It will simply not be worth it. Where Christianity is only one religion among many, there will be little advantage in being Christian. Although Christians will always encourage others in the faith, there will no longer be strong familial and national ties to Christianity.

Men and women will be Christian because they freely choose to be so. It will require total dedication since it will be much easier not to be Christian. It will have to be worked at. Christians will be actively such; passive Christianity will be a thing of the past.

Old and New

The Charismatic Renewal is both old and new. It is old in its traditional beliefs and values: the Holy Spirit, gifts, use of Scripture, sense of community, etc. It is new, at least for Catholics, in its particular style of piety.

While its basic values belong to all Christians, this style of piety does not appeal to all Christians. This is as it should be, for the Church has always fostered and encouraged a pluralism of ascetical and devotional approaches: Carmelite, Franciscan, Dominican, Ignatian, etc.

Modern Appeal

Without prejudice, however, to any one of these styles of Christian life, I think that there are certain aspects in the approach of the Charismatic Renewal which make it especially fitting and appealing in our day:

Constitutive of Church

1. The charismatic dimension of Christian life is a constitutive element both of the Church itself and of Christian spirituality. It is not, as are the others, an emphasis on one or another virtue of a fully developed Christian spirituality.

Belongs to All Christians

2. The Renewal is, I truly believe, more directly the work of the Spirit in the total Church. Religious Orders came from the inspiration, example, and genius of individual Christians to meet the particular needs of their age.

Fits Present Needs

3. The Charismatic Renewal responds most fittingly to the needs and values of contemporary man. These are also the values emphasized by Vatican II. They are especially: acknowledgement of the important place of the individual Christian in the life of the Church; participation in all levels of the work of the Church, etc.

Integration

The Charismatic Renewal will have served its purpose when it ceases to exist as a distinct and novel devotional style and becomes integrated into ordinary, everyday Christian life. A comparison with the liturgical movement is appropriate. For when those goals for which that movement strove were incorporated in theory and in practice into the ordinary liturgical life of the Church, then it ceased to be a distinct movement affecting only a portion of Christians.

Only Acceptable Direction

In a similar way the Charismatic Renewal will have served its purpose when it becomes integrated into the total life of the Church. This is the only acceptable direction for the Renewal, for the charismatic (gift) dimension is essential to the Church and belongs to the normal spiritual life of every Christian.

Within Framework of Church

It follows that, if it is to continue as a Renewal, it must do so within the framework of the existing Church. It must relate itself to and lend its insights, practices and strengths to all the other areas and dimensions of the Body of Christ: the sacramental, the hierarchical, the doctrinal, the ascetical, the devotional, etc. It must do this, too, within the present geographical structure of diocese, parish, etc., for this is where the Church exists primarily today.

Two-Way Responsibility

The responsibility for this renewal rests upon all Christians, those who attend prayer-meetings and those who do not. Those who are involved in the Renewal must guard against elitism. *All* Christians are charismatic by baptism. They should avoid applying the adjective "charismatic" to some Christians as distinct from others. Many cannot and should not deny the great benefits they have received through the Renewal. Their attitude toward others should be, in effect: "I don't feel that I am better than you are; but I know I am better than I was."

Reaching Out

On the other hand, those who themselves do not feel drawn toward prayer-groups should still reach out to those who are and help them to enjoy their birthright as Christians.

Leadership of Priests

The Charismatic Renewal deserves much more than the "hands off," "let's wait and see" attitude of those whose support it needs so greatly. Prayer-groups are springing up everywhere. In order to be properly integrated into parochial and diocesan life, they need the leadership of priests, as our bishops have said. They explicitly encouraged priests to become involved.

Priests Profit Greatly

Priests attest, almost without exception, to the immense personal benefits they derive from the Renewal. Many have said that their spiritual lives have been radically changed for the better; some have said that their priestly ministry has been restored; some, that they would most likely have left the active ministry except for the Renewal.

I believe that any priest who attends a prayer-meeting should do so primarily to praise Jesus with fellow-Christians and to share equally with them his

God-given gifts. With all my heart I encourage my fellow-priests to attend and to share with others their humanity, their Christianity and their priesthood, in that order. In so doing, one's priesthood loses nothing; rather, he will see it greatly respected and enhanced.

Man Among Men

At meetings a priest will find that he is among men and women who have all the virtues and all the weaknesses of any group of Christians. He, like Jesus, will be among sinners. He will share his sinfulness and strength mutually with them—to heal and be healed in turn. He will know a relationship with Jesus and with fellow-Christians that can be found in few other areas of priestly ministry. Like hundreds of priests I have met, he will look back gratefully to the day he first sat down at a prayer-meeting, as I do myself. Praise God!